N

RUSSIA

AUSTRIA /
HUNGARY

ROMANIA

Black Sea

SERBIA

BULGARIA

The Bosphorus

ALBANIA

Constantinople

Sea of Marmara

Salonika

Imbros

Tenedos

OTTOMAN EMPIRE

Lemnos

Gallipoli Peninsula and Dardanelles

GREECE

Aegean Sea

CYPRUS

CRETE

Mediterranean Sea

Alexandria

0   Miles   200

Suez Canal

EGYPT

The Gallipoli Peninsula, The Dardanelles, The Balkans and The Eastern
Mediterranean 1915.

GALLIPOLI 1915
Pens, Pencils and
Cameras at War

ALSO AVAILABLE FROM BRASSEY'S

GODDEN
Harrier: Ski-jump to Victory

LIDDLE
Home Fires and Foreign Fields

MYLES
Jump Jet, 2nd Edition

RUSI
RUSI/Brassey's Defence Yearbook, 1985

SIMPKIN
Race to the Swift
Red Armour

SORRELS
US Cruise Missile Programs: Development, Deployment
and Implications for Arms Control

WINDASS
Avoiding Nuclear War: Common Security as a Strategy for the
Defence of the West

GALLIPOLI 1915

Pens, Pencils and Cameras at War

by

Peter H. Liddle

BRASSEY'S DEFENCE PUBLISHERS
a Member of the Pergamon Group

LONDON · OXFORD · WASHINGTON D.C. · NEW YORK
TORONTO · SYDNEY · PARIS · FRANKFURT

U.K.	Brassey's Defence Publishers Ltd., Maxwell House, 74 Worship Street, London EC2A 2EN, England
U.S.A.	Pergamon-Brassey's International Defense Publishers, 1340 Old Chain Bridge Road, McLean, VA 22101, USA
CANADA	Pergamon Press Canada Ltd., Suite 104, 150 Consumers Road, Willowdale, Ontario M2J 1P9, Canada
AUSTRALIA	Pergamon Press (Aust.) Pty. Ltd., P.O. Box 544, Potts Point, N.S.W. 2011, Australia
FRANCE	Pergamon Press SARL, 24 rue des Ecoles, 75240 Paris, Cedex 05, France
FEDERAL REPUBLIC OF GERMANY	Pergamon Press GmbH, Hammerweg 6, D-6242 Kronberg-Taunus, Federal Republic of Germany

Copyright © 1985 Peter H. Liddle

First edition 1985

Library of Congress Cataloging in Publication Data
Liddle, Peter.
Gallipoli 1915.
1. World War, 1914–1918 — Campaigns — Turkey —
Gallipoli Peninsula. 2. World War, 1914–1918 — Personal
narratives. 3. Gallipoli Peninsula (Turkey) — History.
I. Title
D568.2.L49 1985   940.4'26   84–28509

British Library Cataloguing in Publication Data
Liddle, Peter, 1934–
Gallipoli 1915: pens, pencils and cameras at war.
1. World War, 1914–1918 — Campaigns — Turkey
— Gallipoli Peninsula
I Title
940.4'25   D568.3
ISBN 0-08-031172-5

Printed in Great Britain by A. Wheaton & Co. Ltd., Exeter

Acknowledgements

This book is respectfully dedicated to the memory of all who served in the Gallipoli campaign. I am, of course, in particular mindful of those whose documentation, drawn from my 1914–18 personal experience archives, has been selected for inclusion in the book. Their names are appropriately noted by each illustration.

I would like to add that I could not have devoted the time necessary for the preparation of the book without the generous and talented help of the men and women who have assisted, and who continue to assist, in the many tasks required in the administration of the archives. A distinguished New Zealand Professor of History visiting Sunderland said he had never seen in his academic experience a team quite like it, so committed to voluntary work, and I am fully aware of the privilege I enjoy in having such support.

I am grateful to Kathleen Barnes who has typed the text of the book, to Colin Jones, who with Albert Snell, Headmaster of Heworth Grange Comprehensive School, has copied the photographs and documents and to David Dickinson of Pergamon Press whose design flair has shaped the book. Above all I am grateful to my wife Louise who has helped in so many ways with archive work, listening patiently to what I have written, making constructive suggestions about it and about photograph selection, but most supportive of all, by bringing sunshine into every day.

Dipity Cottage, Waldridge Fell,   PETER H. LIDDLE, F.R.Hist.S.
County Durham, 1984

Contents

Gallipoli 1915: Pens, pencils and cameras at war

Such is the undiminished fascination of all aspects of the Gallipoli campaign that it is somewhat startling to remind oneself that 1985 sees the 70th anniversary of British and Commonwealth troops being towed onto the beaches for their assault upon the Peninsula in 1915. The landing and the campaign which ensued became so enshrined in Australian and New Zealand history that clearly they played a significant part in forging their self-confident identity as independent nations. By a striking parallel the same might be said for modern Kemalist Turkey which emerged from the cocoon of the Ottoman Empire. It has not been solely in those countries that the Gallipoli experience has left a lasting mark, for it is noteworthy that as late as 1967 there was founded in the United Kingdom an association of old comrades who served on the Peninsula or in the Dardanelles in 1915.

Happily there are still alive today numbers of men whose recall of facets of their service has a convincing timbre of truth. This book attempts to set out the contemporary evidence of participants in order to reveal that there was something unique about their service, perceived at the time as especial, and which in its separate elements has been recalled by many of them years later with something not far short of relish.

A compound of emotions is bound up in such a revelation, but there are sound historical reasons which explain why the campaign continues to hold the interest of those who examine political and military planning in war, those who evaluate the performance of High Command and those who seek to enquire into the behaviour of men under the stress of active service. It is ironic and fortunate that the inefficiency of 1915 security measures to prevent the use of private cameras, the keeping of diaries and adequately to censor letters has allowed the accumulation of a rich source of evidence from which an attempt can be made to isolate the character of service in this great enterprise.

Some of the most dominant ingredients of the essence of Gallipoli may seem at first to be outside the range of understanding of those who actually participated in the campaign, but there is evidence to suggest that such an assumption would be too sweeping. There was some awareness in the Mediterranean Expeditionary Force that an assault on the Peninsula to secure the Dardanelles was a huge gamble, that it would test naval and army planning organisation and performance in new ways, but that there was the real possibility of a swift victory which would have a major effect upon the course of the whole war. There was a palpable understanding that great things were needed and expected.

Certainly no one can have been unaware that the forces involved contained new and unusual combinations. Well before 25 April it was clear that seaplanes, ships and soldiers were to operate together in ways hitherto unexplored. The seaplanes may have attracted comment in a midshipman's diary because of their novelty rather than through the young officer's realisation of their utility, but there is no question of the inspiration which uplifted the soldier as his troopship found anchorage in Mudros Bay, just one vessel in a vast armada of shipping for a combined operation on an enormous scale.

It was clear too that in striking contrast to the Western Front there was in the Eastern Mediterranean to be British rather than French leadership in Anglo-French co-operation. Initially this was the case with the naval operations, but then it was to continue in just as successful a vein in the military campaign. By no means was this the limit of the degree of national and indeed racial co-operation obvious to all. The French troops included Algerians, Moroccans and Senegalese with their distinctive appearance and uniform, a whole sector of the landings was to be undertaken by Australian and New Zealand troops and among the latter, Maoris were to play a noteworthy part as the campaign developed. There were soldiers from the Indian subcontinent, Newfoundlanders, an Independent Zionist Mule Corps, and many of these units were to serve alongside battalions with strong national or regional identity from all parts of the British Isles.

This marvellously mixed force was to serve on what was, spacially, a tiny stage of the Classical world. The siege of the new objectives took place within twentieth-century shell shot across the Dardanelles from the ancient ruins of the beleagured Troy of King Priam. Indeed the troops of the Mediterranean Expeditionary Force might attack with the weapons of the modern industrial world, but they would face the age-old universal enemies of the soldier, extremes of climate, the related problems of health, the prevention of disease, the treatment of wounds and the maintenance of morale under conditions of prolonged military stalemate.

To attempt to grasp just how restricted was the area of the fighting it is useful to consider what had been won before the evacuations took place. Three beachheads were created in the course of the campaign. At the tip of the Peninsula, at Cape Helles, an advance was made of just over three miles on what was, at the widest distance from the northern cliffs of the Peninsula south to the shores of the Dardanelles, a front of two miles. At what became known as the Anzac beachhead, the area won was a good deal less and at the third sector, Suvla Bay, an advance of about three miles was made from the head of the bay, the advance at its widest being on a six-mile front. From all points of view this is sobering. To read what was claimed in the War Council as the fruits to be anticipated from success, to consider the material and manpower investment in the campaign and the political, military and human cost of failure; make the knowledge of the inconsequentiality and short-lived nature of the bitterly gained footholds stick in the mind with about as little comfort as a fishbone in the throat.

Still further to delineate what was distinctive about Gallipoli and known at the time to be distinctive, no single part of the confined Allied-held positions was secure from shell fire, and yet within those cramped exposed areas, attack and defence had to be planned and carried out, supplies accumulated and distributed, communications maintained, troop movements concealed, bomb factories and bombing schools run, casualty clearing stations and regimental aid posts set up and even a primitive airfield at Helles established. If football were played at Helles with necessary intervals for enemy shellfire, then more extraordinary still in view of the terrain, cricket was played at Anzac. There was a canteen at Helles and at Anzac a YMCA tent with a piano. There were water-purifying plants and even at Anzac a narrow gauge railway. Motorbikes were used at Suvla and one was photographed in a communication trench at Helles, presumably operating more effectively there than the few armoured cars landed at the tip of the Peninsula. It all makes up a singularly unusual picture to which may be added the essential operations of horse-drawn field ambulances, some motor lorries and the trundling of a traction engine.

It may not come readily to mind that with few exceptions no fit man departed the Peninsula on leave and no base areas on the lines of those behind the Western Front allowed for safe recreation, retraining and rehabilitation. No nurses in the field hospitals were there to represent the fairer sex, the female vision existing solely in the mind or in the correspondence of the Gallipoli soldier.

Of the actual fighting, there was much that would be familiar to the few who had served in France. Trench warfare at Helles and Suvla, except in the relative lack of supporting artillery, was in no fundamental way different from that in Flanders, but at Anzac things were different. Such was the nature of the ground that linked dugouts and covered galleries open to the seaward side were set into the face of precipices, reached only by near vertical steps cut into the face of the cliff. Trenches were actually blocked by sandbags, the separated sections held by opposing forces either side of the barrier; sheer ravines, bare slopes and others thickly overgrown with stunted trees and prickly bush gave a character to the fighting which cannot be paralleled by any other 1914–18 campaigning conditions faced by the British soldier, and certainly they were quite different from those which confronted him in mountainous country in Italy in late 1917 and 1918.

The climate and the confined area of the fighting made their own special contribution to the moulding of the Gallipoli experience. The incidence of dysentery was a scourge comparable to that of malaria in Macedonia. Heat, flies, a narrow no-man's-land, difficulty over the burial of men and mules, providing for covered latrines and for waste disposal, became exceptionally severe trials for which other fighting fronts provide no real parallel.

There are other factors which combine to ensure that Gallipoli refuses to fade from the national conscience, factors like the way in which the concept of operations evolved (something which in fact probably stifled at birth the prospect of success), the question of political responsibility for an enterprise which ended so ignominiously, and the merit or otherwise of naval and military leadership. There are, however, two further and quite outstanding linked elements which should ensure that Gallipoli continues to hold a place of honour as long as military endeavour is judged worthy of examination: the sheer drama of the six separate beach landings on 25 April and the sustained tension of the brilliantly successful evacuation in December and then in January 1916. If all this were not sufficient in establishing a case extraordinary in many of its component parts, then what other Allied campaign in the First World War was conceived, planned, launched, maintained, reinforced and then abandoned all inside a year?

Rather than dilate upon the chameleon-like character of the Gallipoli concept[1], I would like to provide a framework for this book by highlighting the successive stages at which the Turk was challenged. The stages will each be represented later in the book by the personal testimony of men who were there.

In November 1914 British ships shelled the outer forts of the Dardanelles and in so doing rang an aggressive tocsin which surprisingly was followed by no further measures nor, more surprisingly still, by any vigorous Turkish defensive precautions, though the Turks were proven masters at entrenchment and the stubborn holding of such emplacements.

With stalemate on the Western Front, the fertile imagination of Winston Churchill, First Lord of the Admiralty, and of others in the War Council too, was given free rein by a January 1915 Russian plea for an Allied move to divert the Turk from his campaign on the Russo-Turkish front in the Caucasus. Top level debate was influenced towards acquiescence in a Dardanelles gamble by three factors above all: first, by the current deadlock on the Western Front which provided the tempting delusion that something different would be something better; second, by the wide-ranging political and military benefits claimed as attendant consequences upon success in the venture (though this was based on a "logical" progression which satisfies no one today); and third, by the sheer

[1]See *Home Fires and Foreign Fields*, ed. P. H. Liddle, Brassey's, 1985.

economy of the means declared necessary to give effect to the grand design.

As for this economy, the logic behind it seems to be that which disarmingly persuades so many to buy on the doorstep something which is in fact a good deal dearer than is apparent from the way in which it is temptingly presented. In short, the reasoning was that there was no hope of an early end to the deadlock in France, but the defeat of the Turks would assist Russia, save Serbia, bring Italy, Bulgaria and Romania to the Allied fold, threaten the heartland of the Habsburg Empire by means of a (miraculous) challenge up the Danube, secure Suez, safeguard India and the oil of the Persian Gulf, divert German resources from the Western Front and allow for the increased deployment of Allied resources there in such a way as to make a breakthrough possible. Furthermore, all this would be achieved by the limited use of a number of old ships steadily bombarding the forts, the guns of which defended the minefields of the Narrows. The minefields would be swept, then, taking and (somehow) holding the Gallipoli Peninsula, the Eastern Mediterranean Squadron would proceed through to the Sea of Marmara and thence to the Golden Horn. The appearance of the ships off Constantinople would promote capitulation, or revolution and capitulation, and so the key moves on the international chess board of war would be made or forced.

With the prospect of the resolution of such problems and the making of such enormous gains by so limited an investment, the War Council was not distinguished by those emulating doubting Thomas. The only soul in whom alarm bells rang early, took refuge in sulky official silence, though in correspondence and conversation the man concerned, Sir John Fisher, the First Sea Lord, erupted in veritably volcanic character.

From 19 February and into early March the ships bombarded the forts and shore parties were landed for demolition work. Minesweeping with inadequate vessels proceeded. The work was slow and dangerous and the results inconclusive. The shore parties too met increasing opposition. On 18 March the old battleships, working to a careful plan but a plan which rightly protected the splendid reinforcement of the new 15-inch gun *Queen Elizabeth*, entered the Narrows for close range bombardment. A newly laid line of mines accounted for one French and two British ships, others being very seriously damaged. The day was a tragic one for the Allies, its outcome soberly captured in an officer's letter home: "the day was far from a victory for us".

Whatever the arguments for resumption of the attack in the belief that the Turks were almost out of ammunition and that revolution was stirring in Constantinople, unsuitable weather closed down any such possibility for the moment and a conference of the two very recently appointed naval and military commanders was held. The officers in command were Vice-Admiral J. M. de Robeck of the Eastern Mediterranean Squadron and General Sir Ian Hamilton commanding the cosmopolitan Mediterranean Expeditionary Force being assembled in the Middle East for some sort of support for the naval efforts. They decided upon a combined operation to effect landings upon the Peninsula. They had little enough time for preparation. Much went wrong, but much was accomplished. With the shelling, the continued naval presence, the assembling of thousands of troops, the great number of troopships and naval vessels in the main bay of Lemnos Island some forty miles from the entrance to the Dardanelles and with reconnaissance of the beaches from both sea and air, the one thing which had been lost beyond recall was surprise. As the combined force concentrated upon the Island of Lemnos, an artillery officer, Guy Walford, left testimony that he had no illusions about the consequences which would now be faced by the soldiers. He was neither a Jeremiah in private nor a Duke of Plazatoro in public: he and another officer led men with selfless courage to clear the castle and fort above one landing beach and were killed in so doing.

The Turks, under German command, had worked belatedly but effectively in the priceless few weeks they had before the onslaught. When it came on 25 April they had done much to justify the unconcealed forebodings in the 29th Divisional Commander's personal message to his troops just before the great day.

Sir Ian Hamilton's plan boldly defied an accepted military principle by dispersing his own resources in order to prevent Turkish concentration against any of his landings. The task he had to fulfil demanded the securing of the Narrows, so Cape Helles had to be the main objective, thus eliminating the one area, Suvla Bay, where his force of over 70,000 could have been landed in a single concentration. A temporary landing on the Asiatic shore, a diversion further south and one in the north off the celebrated lines of Bulair were designed to deny any opportunity for the Turks to oppose in strength the five separate landings at Cape Helles by the 29th, a Regular Army division, and the landing to be made by the Australian and New Zealand troops just north of a headland called Gaba Tepe. Men from the Royal Naval Division fulfilled different roles in their dispersal between the Bulair diversion, the Gaba Tepe and Cape Helles landings.

The tows of launches and cutters filled with Australian troops being drawn to the shore by steam picket boats, then cast off to be rowed the last yards towards the beach, were the first to alert the Turks. Navigational error in the dark had brought the Australians in further north than had been the intention. This was to be at one and the same time a curse and a blessing. Fearsome terrain was to be faced, quite impossible for a co-ordinated advance led by whatever dash. As one man wrote at the time: "Men of all units were mixed up, command as far as orders were concerned was lost. There was one yell and a rush towards the cliff . . . shouting like demons." The vital third ridge which commanded the approach to the Dardanelles shoreline could not be taken and held. Isolated small groups which had made fine progress towards key points were forced back or were captured or died in their attempt to hold on. For those men unwounded and for the supporting troops, if there were determination to stay and dig in, there was cover from which it would be as difficult to turn them out as it was for those who dug in to make further advance. The position was precarious, but the Commander-in-Chief's decision to refuse the withdrawal request made by the Brigade Commanders ashore was surely right. The beachhead was held, disaster was averted. What had been achieved was far short of the high hopes entertained, but things might have been very much worse.

At Helles, troops were put ashore at the foot of cliffs at two points on the northern shore of the Peninsula, Y and X beaches. At the tip of the Peninsula, against gentler slopes, further landings were made: W beach, small, fronting low cliffs, and then further south V beach below a medieval castle and its attendant village of Seddul Bahr. A final landing to outflank Seddul Bahr was made within the mouth of the Narrows at Morto Bay, S beach.

The high point of tactical interest concerns the most northerly landing at Y beach. An advance from the cliffs here could have taken the village of Krithia in the rear and allowed for an attempt to take the one dominant height which commanded all the local terrain, a 700-foot hill called Achi Baba. The advance was not made, the Turks came up in strength and the tiny clifftop perimeter had to be evacuated. Perhaps more was lost than Y beachhead itself.

Of heroism and tragic drama, the deeds of the Lancashire Fusiliers at W beach, where a footing at great cost was secured, and then the events at V beach together provide imperishable evidence. A fusilier who was towed and then rowed onto W beach recalled that in his boat "people to right and left of me were killed almost at once, but we were so tightly packed that until we reached the shore it was difficult to tell who was hit as neither dead nor alive could move much".

Just a few miles from the Asiatic shore site of the original Trojan horse, a modern version, the collier *River Clyde*, with two thousand troops in her holds, was run into the shingle of V beach. She was towing a hopper and lighters which were heroically manhandled to form a bridge across the shallows from the ship to the shore. The troops, with others ferried in by tows, faced devastating fire from Turkish positions insufficiently damaged by naval shelling. The castle and the village were taken, but the red-stained sea and the unburied dead starkly revealed the cost in death of winning such immortality. One man may speak for many in recording that for those landing at V beach later in the day when the Turkish fire had been reduced: "the most dreadful thing was having to walk on the dead both in the barges and between the barges and the beach".

Battles at Anzac and Helles in April and May, then in June and July at Helles, sought to throw the invaders out or break the will of the defender. Sunscorched deadlock was the sour fruit of all endeavour. Only in the achievement of British and Australian submarines was the Turk harassed in the Marmara and in fact even in the waters off Constantinople too. At Anzac the smell of the dead after the breaking of successive waves of Turkish attack in May led of necessity to a truce for burial, but the spirit of the Turks who survived must have been raised on the day following when in clear sight of attackers and defenders the old British battleship *Triumph* was torpedoed. Two days later British troops at Helles saw another old battleship torpedoed off W beach and the remaining great grey ships sailed away to safety from the submarine scourge, lowering the spirits of the men in khaki who had no such safe refuge except by the uncertain fate of wound or disability.

Major reinforcement in midsummer encouraged Sir Ian Hamilton to produce an imaginative plan for an August breakout from his trapped positions at Anzac. With diversionary attacks at Helles and on the right flank at Anzac, a new landing at Suvla Bay was to strike quickly inland to win heights which would outflank the Turks and support a move on the left of the Anzac position where a night march north along the beach would split into a three-armed silent advance up unreconnoitred gullies leading to the heights which could not be stormed frontally.

Weak, then misguided, leadership at Suvla, awesome terrain at Anzac, shrewdly bold Turkish generalship and not least the drained tiredness of many of the units used in the Anzac breakout, led to frustration again. It is just possible that local success lay within reach at Anzac, but that remains an intriguing hypothesis. The delayed advance from Suvla Bay simply won more ground to be overlooked by the Turkish positions.

Autumn deadlock succeeded that of the summer. A new Commander-in-Chief, Sir Charles Munro, replaced the man who remains one of the paradoxes of 1914–18 High Command: a general with good pre-1914 experience, a thinking, imaginative, optimistic, personally brave commander who somehow lacked the special military yeast to rise to the occasion; it may be added sympathetically in parenthesis that the occasion was half-baked too!

Kitchener himself visited the Peninsula at the beginning of November, his visit confirming in his mind the wisdom of the new Commander-in-Chief that an evacuation must be carried through. Late in November the weather dealt a cruel blow in every sense. A storm of wind, rain, snow and freezing temperatures actually drowned and froze men to death. First the rain and floods filling the Suvla trenches, as if by a "tidal wave" as an official report recorded, then the snow and terrible cold, numbing both the physical capacity and the will towards movement and self-preservation. Two hundred and eight deaths, sixteen thousand cases of frostbite and exposure reflect a picture of unrelieved misery. The ill wind did, however, usefully blow away the last London and Peninsula objections to the need for evacuation.

Meticulous plans were laid. Ways were found to deceive the Turks, first about the progressive reduction of the numbers of troops occupying the Allied positions and then, more important still, about the actual departure of all the men left at Anzac and Suvla. In a two-night operation in the third week of December, with no seeming diminution of normal trench-holding activity, everyone was safely evacuated. "The twenty-six of us who remained went from firing bay to firing bay trying to keep up a normal firing rate. I placed a box of ammunition in the cookhouse fire hoping it would last till we left. At 3 a.m. we crept silently away. The silence could be felt and as we approached the beachhead many glances were cast behind us, not, I believe, in fear of the Turks but as a goodbye to Suvla Bay, all its memories and the friends we were leaving behind." There had been no "crowding in the boats of thousands of half crazy men, the swamping of craft, the nocturnal panic, the hecatombs of the slain", as had been forecast in a memorandum to the War Council by Lord Curzon, Secretary of State for India, but that a similar operation in the face of more vigorous Turkish activity was also successful at Helles in early January was nothing short of astonishing. Bulgaria's late October entry into the war on the side of the Central Powers had greatly facilitated German aid to Turkey. A massacre on the evacuation beaches as troops were being withdrawn was a real possibility. It did not take place, and this redounds to the credit of the High Command and to that of all the officers, N.C.O.s and men of the reduced Mediterranean Expeditionary Force.

The campaign was over, the substance of a new saga of human endeavour laid down. Here in Britain we seem to choose to celebrate our defeats as well as our victories, and in this fashion Gallipoli has secured its niche in an honourable tradition. The tradition may predate Boadicea, include the Battle of Hastings and clearly it may not end with Dunkirk or Arnhem, but about Gallipoli there will always hang an aura of very special human endeavour in most extraordinary, pitiful and tragic circumstances. If this book, in letting men who were there speak for themselves, were to evoke a telling picture of those circumstances and recapture that aura, it will have succeeded in its aim.

In the beginning

S.M.S. *Goeben*, the German battle cruiser, arriving at Constantinople in August 1914 having evaded British interception. The Gallipoli campaign had its practical origins in the late October shelling of Russian Black Sea ports by *Goeben*, the light cruiser *Breslau* and Turkish ships. In a retaliatory demonstration, British warships shelled the forts at the entrance to the Dardanelles.

J. W. WHITTALL

"Stills" from a ciné film of *Goeben* in 1972 just before she was broken up in a Turkish naval base.

DEMONSTRATION BY BOMBARDMENT
OF DARDANELLES.

·········

"INDEFATIGABLE",

2nd. November 1914.

No. 019D.   MEMORANDUM.

A demonstration bombardment will take place at
daylight about 4.15 a.m. on Tuesday, 3rd. November 1914.

2.   Ships taking part will be those of the 1st.
and 2nd. Divisions of the Detached Squadron.

3.   "Indefatigable" will fire at Fort No. 3
SEDDUL BAHR.
        "Indomitable" will fire at Fort No. 5 SEDDUL BAHR.
        The French ships will fire at KUM KALESSI - on the
south side of the entrance.

4.   The range will be approximately 14000 to
12000 yards, bearing as in the plan attached; speed of ships
will be 15 knots.

5.   Ships are not to fire more than eight rounds
per turret unless otherwise ordered by signal.
        Full charges and common shell.

6.   Rapidity of fire is necessary in this
operation, as it is desirable to keep the ships engaged
undamaged if possible.

7.   Should the forts reply the ships will turn
together by signal before the fire from the forts becomes
effective.

*verité will
probably fire
8" guns .
S.K.*

S.H.Carden

VICE ADMIRAL.

The Rear Admiral Commanding
        Second Division
and the Commanding Officers,
        H.M.Ships concerned.

Orders for the 3 November 1914 demonstration bombardment of the
outer forts of the Dardanelles.

REAR ADMIRAL P. GUÉPRATTE
(*In Command of the Squadron of French ships*)

H. M. Submarine B XI

M. D. S.

Jan 4th 1915.

My dear Admiral Guépratte.

    I am writing to thank you very much for your kind letter of congratulations. It is impossible for me to tell you how much I appreciate receiving such a letter, especially from the admiral of our most noble allies. It is most gracious of you to have written to the Commander-in-Chief about me, & should the Government of the French Republic confer upon me that high distinction, the Legion of Honour, I shall be one of the proudest officers in His Majesties Navy. I am afraid the small service I have done is not worthy of such high distinction.

    Again I thank you with all my heart for your great kindness to me.

        Believe me
          Yours Very Sincerely
          Norman. D. Holbrook.
            Lieut-in-Command
            H. M. Sub. B XI

A British submarine commander, having successfully torpedoed the Turkish battleship *Messudieh* in Sari Siglar Bay on 13 December 1914, acknowledges French congratulations. N. D. Holbrook's success earned him the Victoria Cross, the first naval V.C. in the war to be gazetted.

REAR ADMIRAL P. GUÉPRATTE

Unknowingly en route for the Dardanelles

Of the allied contingents which would serve in the Gallipoli Campaign Australian and New Zealand troops were the first to leave their homeland for a voyage which would take them to the Middle East.

This photograph shows some Australian troops, not in the first contingent to leave, but still, in fact, encamped at Broadmeadows, Melbourne, in December 1914.

L to R. Alec Higgins, Curly Young (lying down), Bill Davies, a visitor, Sam Norris, Bill Hartigan (seated), Fred and Jack.

S. NORRIS
(Pte. 6th Bn. A.I.F.)

New Zealanders of the 1st N.Z. Expeditionary Force embark at Lyttelton
in September 1914.

O. L. WATSON
(Pte. 1st Bn. Canterbury Regiment)

ANSON BATTALION,
ROYAL NAVAL [...]
BLANDFORD,
DORSET.

22.2.15.

Dear Irene,

We are off at last. Tuesday we draw equipment, Wednesday parade before [Winston Churchill] & an Thursday march off to some seaport & ship for the Mediterranean. We have been promised a six-week or two-month campaign, probably fairly exciting, & then we'll come back refit & go to the continent with the whole division. At present only 7 battalions are going, the howitzer brigade & the engineers & the remaining infantry battalions aren't ready yet. We are all getting pith helmets. The men are wild with joy.

Since my last letter we have been living the same dull life in camp & it has been getting worse & worse. The mud gets deeper & deeper, & the work less & less interesting: the officers get into quarrels with each other, the commanding [...]

February 1915: the Royal Naval Division learns that the mud of Blandford is to be left for a "six week or two month campaign, probably fairly exciting".

The officer writing this letter was to be killed on 6 May leading his men at the 2nd battle of Krithia, but his fearless attempt to get wounded men off V beach on 25 April was to result in a posthumously awarded Victoria Cross.

A. W. St. C. Tisdall

REGENT HOTEL,

ROYAL LEAMINGTON SPA.

March 15th, 1915.

Never any time to write. Two trains have gone this afternoon; I have just seen the second one off and am writing this before washing for dinner.

~~Whenever~~ This is a very fine Division, the best we have now I think, and we have a very big job to do. If all goes well, we ought to do as much towards settling the war as any other part of the British Army. I am very glad to belong to it and to have such a fine job. I shall be leaving here on Thursday with the General and we sail on Saturday. The 29th Div. Artillery is

A very proper pride in a Regular Army Division, the 29th. The Brigade Major of the 29th Division Artillery writes from Divisional Headquarters to tell his wife that the Division is going overseas: "We have a very big job to do." This officer would earn a posthumously awarded V.C. on the second day of the landing. In a letter written on 6 April he accepted that: "We have got a difficult job in front of us, so you mustn't expect too much at first. The Turks have had full warning thanks to the Navy's trying to do things off their own bat before they had any land forces to work with them, and the Germans are said to have sent a lot of guns, officers and men to stiffen the Turkish Army."

CAPT. G. N. WALFORD V.C.

Ritual celebrations as a New Zealand troop ship crosses the Equator.

O. L. WATSON
(Pte. 1st Bn. Canterbury Regiment, N.Z.E.F.)

Dry (very dry!) land at last.
The land of the Pharaohs
reached

Outside Mena Camp: Australians before making their own history!

Source unknown

The Australian 1st Division camp at Mena.

S. NORRIS
(Pte. 6th Bn. A.I.F.)

Gurkhas and New Zealanders getting to know each other at Ismailia, Egypt.

A. E. ROBINSON
(Pte. 1st Bn. Auckland Regiment, N.Z.E.F.)

Australians in Cairo *en route* in February to the railway station and temporary duty at El Kantara to face a Turkish threat to the Suez Canal.

A. E. JONES
(Cpl. 7th Bn. A.I.F.)

New Zealanders improvise thorough ablutions at Ismailia, Egypt.

GEORGE MAY
(Sgt. 1st Bn. Auckland Regiment, N.Z.E.F.)

Royal Naval Division officers finding few thoroughbred mounts for polo in Egypt.

W. E. Bland
(R.N.D. Nelson Battalion)

(3)

I would like to send you more.

I went into Cairo with Bob. Edwards on Thursday to get a couple of teeth stopped. We also went to see the mosque of Mohammid Ali the first Khedive of Egypt. It was built 120 years ago & is the finest in the world, I do wish you could see it, it is lovely; the main hall is lit by 700 lights.

When the architect had finished it the Khedive ordered his hands to be cut off & his eyes burnt out so that he could not build another like it, grateful wasn't he.

There was a riot in the streets of Cairo in the evening & a few soldiers were shot although none were killed, It is a great pity it happened, it will get us a bad name all over the world, but they have been bottled up here so long & were rather excited at the prospect of getting away, still that does not excuse them.

I did all my washing this afternoon so as to have so many clean clothes as possible to go away with

We had church parade on Good-Friday morning but no hot X buns

I hope we get another mail before we get away, we might get one at Alexandria.

I hope you are all well at home & not worrying too much.

"It will get us a bad name all over the world." A Tasmanian refers to the "Battle of the Wasser" in which Australian soldiers rioted and caused considerable damage in the brothel area of Cairo.

A. Clennett
(Sgt. 9th Battery Australian Field Artillery
letter from Mena Camp)

"War damage" to red light district of Cairo after some Australian troops had been in action.

F. ROGERS
(Sgt. 1st Otago Battalion N.Z.E.F.)

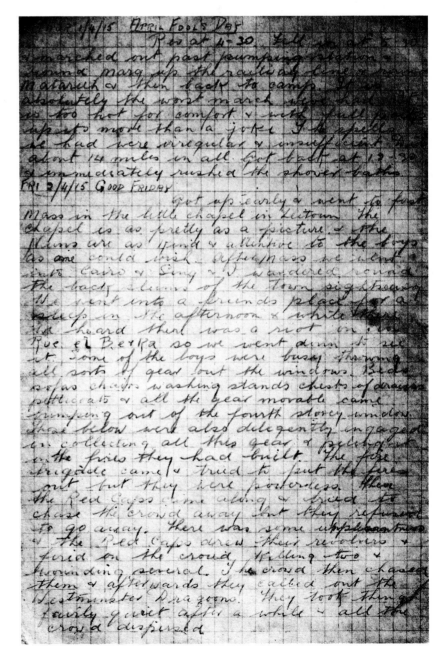

A New Zealander observes the Australians bidding a riotous farewell to Cairo's red light district.

C. J. WALSH
(Pte. 1st Australian Regiment)

Awaiting departure from Alexandria.

R. Howard

Naval bombardment: February and March 1915

February 1915: the French battleship *Suffren* off Tenedos.

J. G. T. Taylor
(Surgeon R.N.V.R.)

Opening Phase of Bombardment of the Dardanelles
February 19th 1915

Fleet taking part consisted of "Inflexible" (Flag of V.A. Carden) "Vengeance" (Flag of V.A. DeRobeck) "Queen Elizabeth" "Agamemnon", "Cornwallis", "Triumph", 4 French Battleships & a Flotilla of our Destroyers ("Beagle" class)

—

At 9.50 am "Cornwallis", steaming approximately NE + S.W. between Seddhul Bahr & Yeni Shehr at a range of about 10,000 yards opened fire on Fort No 5 with her 12" Guns. No reply was received from the Forts.

At 10.0 am "Triumph" opened fire at Forts 1 & 2 at long distant range.

At 10.30 a.m a French battleship anchored under the lee of the land due East of Mavro opened fire on Kum Kalesi.

At 11.0 a.m, accompanied by Flight Commander Williamson, I proceeded in No 172 to control the "Cornwallis" Gun fire. Having climbed to 4000 feet, we found "Cornwallis" had ceased firing so we proceeded to look for mines in the entrance & carry out a general reconnaissance over all the Forts. We saw no sign of mines & found that very slight damage only had been done to the Forts. We dropped one 20 lb. Bomb into No 6 Fort & then landed. On returning to "Ark Royal" we were six times fired at by some Anti-Aircraft guns of an inferior type, between Yeni-Shehr & Yukeri Point. The bombardment continued during the day but nothing of any interest happened until 4.30 P.M. At this time I was away with the "Inflexible" but had to land after climbing to 2000 feet, owing to lack of Petrol. Machines 136 & 922 proceeded on patrol at this time & climbed to 3000 feet, at which height they remained for over an hour carrying out a general reconnaissance over the Forts. Spotting could not be done because all ships were now ordered to fire at the same time.

19 February: an R.N.A.S. seaplane pilot of the seaplane carrier H.M.S. *Ark Royal* observes from the air the opening of the Dardanelles Gallipoli campaign, the naval shelling of the forts guarding the entrance to the Narrows.

AIR VICE MARSHAL SIR G. R. BROMET

19 February: Seddul Bahr at Cape Helles, burning.

P. MAY
(*Leading Seaman. H.M.S. Triumph*)

we were weighing the ship was hit 4 times. At first I experienced the "duck your head" sensation but that very soon wore off and a feeling of exhilaration took its place. I felt as if I did not care a damn what happened next. Out on the F.X. one felt delightfully free and I was not in the least bit of a funk. Burton signalled to the bridge the amount of cable out as it gradually came in. Bishop sitting on the signal bridge trying to hold the two bits of his left leg together repeated them to the fore top. The pluck of that man was marvellous. When the anchor was right up we put on the slip ourselves and then hooked it. I went into the port battery and I saw Bishop being carried below the bottom of his left leg and foot was merely hanging by his sock. His leg was a mass of blood. Not a sound escaped him all the time & after he was wounded he was bright and cheerful and smoked cigarrette immediately after the operation (his leg had to be amputated) to get back. It was such a beastly sight that I went back to the fore turret. Of course all this time we had been firing with our starboard 9.2's. Soon after I got in P.O. Owen came in he had helped to carry Bishop down and he told us that P.O. Worthington had been killed and also Ordinary Seaman Mason. Worsley came into the turret later and we remained closed up until about 10 o'clock. About a quarter to 12 Worsley sent Macleish aft for his pipe & tobacco and when he

25 February: H.M.S. *Agamemnon* is hit as the shelling of the forts is maintained. A midshipman's private diary.

CDR. H. BANKS

Turks in a cemetery. We had some difficulty in finding the point of aim owing to the wrong bearing being passed up. The captain got furious and came and trained the gun himself. He cursed me and told me I ought to have turned the Crael out. It was rather a difficult position.

The Turks were driven off and our marines got back to their boats. I did not expect half necessarily of them to come back. Only 1 was killed and 3 wounded. The one killed I am afraid was mutilated. The Turks vented their whole wrath on him. His head was smashed in, + bullet holes in his face, 1 wrist, 1 shoulder 1 in the knee it was an explosive bullet and had blown his knee cap off. Both his legs were broken and a bayonet wound in his abdomen. One was wounded in the eye and subsequently

had it taken out, one in the shoulder and one in the shin.

The demolition party destroyed four Nordenfeldts at number 6 but did not have time to do anything else. It was very noticeable that all notices and instructions were written in German as well as Turkish.

While the landing party was ashore we went inside. Majestic was hit several times by shots some shore batteries but no damage was done. We were quite close to her at the time. Remained off entrance all night I kept the middle watch.

February 27th Saturday.

Division at 7.0 a.m. and buried Sergeant Turnbull. The service was held in the Starboard battery and he was dropped out of the Sea gangway.

26 February: the grim fate of a Royal Marine from H.M.S. *Vengeance's* fort demolition party. This is from the private diary of a midshipman. Sending ashore parties to complete demolition work was essential because the low trajectory naval shelling was not destroying the guns behind their earthen emplacements.

VICE ADMIRAL SIR PEVERIL WILLIAM POWLETT

A Royal Marine and naval landing party preparing to go ashore from H.M.S. *Irresistible* for fort demolition work.

CDR. R. J. HAYWARD

H.M.S. VENGEANCE

...nes that we could not. On ~~Sunday~~ 25rd we again began. The 'Irresistible' had now arrived and we re yaulois and two other ships lay off and bombarded the entrance forts. The 'Agamemnon' was one of the other ships'. One Turkish fort replied and hit the 'Agamemnon' about 5 times killing 3 and wounding 5. The yaulois was also hit once or twice. After lunch we and the 'Cornwallis' ran in to 3000 yards firing at most of the four forts. After we had come out again 'Suffren' and 'Charlemagne' ran in like us. When they come out the 'Albion' 'Triumph' and us all ran in again and stayed in there smashing up everything. That night we lay outside all night. Houses were blazing all over the place ashore. Several times one of the magazines would blow up with a most awful noise. All the night the mine-sweepers were working up and down sweeping for mines. Next day we again watched the forts to see they did not reply, while destroyers went in to smash up some torpedo tubes. The 'Albion' went

...with the 'Majestic' who had now come right in to take on the next fort. We landed a party to destroy any guns left in Nos 6 and 4 forts, while the 'Irresistible' landed men the other side to put out Nos 3 and 1. Our party smashed up most things except the guns in No 6. A searchlight was also destroyed. We encountered about 30 Turkish snipers, and we lost a marine sergeant killed, and three men wounded. The ship supported with shrapnel and we accounted for a good many Turks. The 'Irresistible' party accounted for No 3 fort.

[censored]

The 'Canopus', 'Ocean' and 'Minerva' have now arrived.

Only 4 mines have been found in the entrance. The accompanying plans may be of interest to you.
Your loving son
...

2 March: bombardment, demolition party landings and mine sweepers: a midshipman's letter gives an account which bears the mark of the censor.

VICE ADMIRAL SIR CHARLES HUGHES HALLETT
(*Midshipman H.M.S. Vengeance*)

Aerial reconnaissance by the Royal Naval Air Service played an important role in the naval operations and then later in preparing for the landings. Here in March, Lieutenant Commander Priston (R.N.: H.M.S. *Prince of Wales*) and Flight Commander Collet, who was to be killed in August, are ready for a flight over the Narrows.

CDR. H. VETCH

18 March 1915: close range naval bombardment and the fateful mines

On 18 March British and French ships entered the Narrows to bombard from close range the forts, the guns of which made mine sweeping so dangerous. Unswept recently laid mines took a heavy toll of allied vessels, two British battleships and one French being lost, while there was serious mine and shell-fire damage to others. Here the new dreadnought battleship H.M.S. *Elizabeth* narrowly escapes Turkish shelling.

CAPT. H. M. DENHAM R.N.
(Midshipman H.M.S. Agamemnon

Still making way as she takes a final plunge in Erenkeui Bay, the mined French battleship *Bouvet* is lost.

CDR. A. G. BUCHANAN

The destroyer H.M.S. *Ribble* carrying survivors of the old battleship *Ocean* which has sunk after striking a mine. *Ribble* is making for the modern battleship H.M.S. *Queen Elizabeth*.

CAPT. H. M. DENHAM R.N

British picket boats and cutters approach the damaged French battleship *Gaulois* to take off many of her crew in case she were to founder, having been seriously damaged in striking a mine.

CONTRE AMIRAL LUCAS
(*Enseigne de Vaisseau Première Classe: Gaulois*)

A few officers and a skeleton crew remain aboard *Gaulois*, the French battleship which was just to reach the Rabbit Islands where she was beached for temporary repair.

CONTRE AMIRAL LUCAS

the gunlayer of the left gun out of action
with splinter wounds it was not very
cheerful in the maintop then to many of
them flying around About that time
3.30 pm the Inflexible caught it properly
her Fore top was smashed in and all
but one in the top being killed, soon after
she was hit on the fore bridge setting it
on fire it was a sight to see her blazing
away & firing her 12" guns the same time,
but that was not the worst that she
was to get for was mined in forward submerged
flat, & 40 hands were killed who were in there
at the time she has The Ocean had the next
billet to the Irresistible but the spot must
have been mined for the Ocean was seen to
have a heavy list & was flying distress signals
& then there was a splendid piece of work done
by the destroyer flotilla they dashed up
through a proper shower of shells & took
everyone off her. The Whaler came for us

A seaman records his view of the events on 18 March: serious damage and casualties for the battle cruiser *Inflexible* and the loss of the two old battleships *Irresistible* and *Ocean*.

G. E. KEELER
(*Seaman. H.M.S. Lord Nelson*)

S.—1320c. (Established—May, 1900.)
(Revised—February, 1914.)

Wardroom

NAVAL SIGNAL.

FROM	To	
V A	Med. Squad Suffren	P.O. OF WATCH.
		READ BY 4
		REPORTED BY
		PASSED BY
		LOGGED BY
		SYSTEM W/T
		DATE 19th
		TIME 6·25 am

The V.A. regrets to announce unfortunate loss by mines of 3 Ships today which he feels was due to no lack of vigilance or forethought on the part of those concerned – We have to regret very serious loss of life in "Bouvet" but in case of other ships it is very small – S.O⁵ of Sub divisions are to prepare their Subs: for further action with as little delay as possible and he knows that everyone will be ready to make further effort and sacrifice where necessary – A means of overcoming difficulties of dealing with floating mines will be found

M. 1704/1900   Stn. 6/14.

[2501] 50,000 pads 8/14.y G & S 3416

Sober reading for the officers of the wardroom of H.M.S. *Ark Royal,* even with the optimistic leavening of "a means of overcoming difficulties of dealing with floating mines will be found".

AIR VICE MARSHAL SIR G. R. BROMET

A gun on the fore shelter deck of H.M.S. *Triumph* after being hit by a shell from the Turkish forts.

P. MAY

An unwelcome disfigurement of the officers' bathroom: H.M.S. *Triumph* after being hit on 18 March.

P. MAY

Shell holes in the quarterdeck of H.M.S. *Triumph* after the action on 18 March. *Triumph* was to be torpedoed by a U boat just over two months later.

P. MAY

From various vantage points H.M.S. *Inflexible*'s damage was serious.

Cdr. C. F. Laborde

The battle cruiser H.M.S. *Inflexible,* which had seen service at the Battle of the Falkland Islands in December 1914 and was to be at Jutland in 1916, was severely damaged by mine and also hit by shellfire on 18 March. Here, in dock at Gibraltar in April, she is undergoing repairs.

REAR ADMIRAL B. SEBASTIAN

Mudros: a combined operation in the offing

Members of the Royal Naval Division have to take to the sea, landing on the island of Lemnos to establish a base by the harbour at Mudros. From here they were to return to Egypt before again making for this Aegean base prior to the Gallipoli landings.

A. GILLOTT
(R.N.D. Engineers)

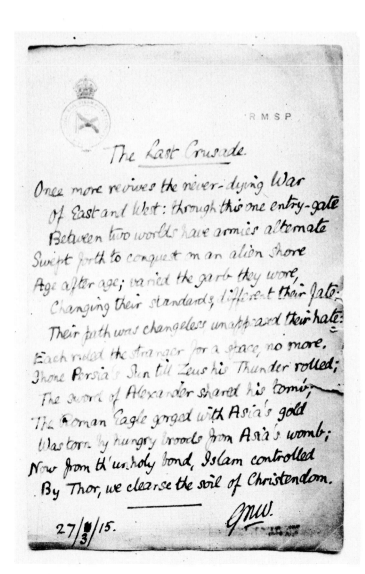

The Last Crusade.

Once more revives the never-dying War
Of East and West: through this one entry-gate
Between two worlds have armies alternate
Swept forth to conquest on an alien shore
Age after age; varied the garb they wore,
Changing their standards, different their fate;
Their path was changeless unabated their hate:
Each ruled the stranger for a space, no more.
Shone Persia's Sun till Zeus his Thunder rolled;
The sword of Alexander shared his tomb;
The Roman Eagle gorged with Asia's gold
Was torn by hungry broods from Asia's womb;
Now from th'unholy bond, Islam controlled
By Thor, we cleanse the soil of Christendom.

G.N.W.

27/3/15.

Captain G. N. Walford who wrote this poem a month before his death at Seddul Bahr was not alone in finding historical inspiration for his theme and for the whole setting and purpose of the Dardanelles enterprise.

CAPT. G. N. WALFORD V.C.

about 140 ships in harbour including French transports

11 LOW SUN — 1 aft Easter Fair sea, sgtl nor. west. 6.45 physical drill
10 am Church service. Noon 8 nom fire alarm

12 MON 8.30 parade in war ... Sea still fair passing islands of Grecian Archi-
peligo small boat. 9.30 practice dis- pelago embarkation with full kits, 2 pm nor
swimmers told off to lifeboats. all rifles cleaned. 7 pm Launch &
boats break away. Cruise ar ound until morning. Strong

13 TUES raining heavily, gig se a running. Launch & boat
jacked up ... 7 am. ... ok sank at 9 am. surf boat
cut adrift & no parades. ... several islands

14 WED 5.30 arrived in King Harbour Lemnos Island. 4.15 pm dropped anchor in
inner harbour. About 25 warships in harbour including torpedo boats, destroy
... submarines & French & Italian warship, also about 30 French & British
transports. Parades disembark... ... & musketry. Queen Elizabeth in harbour

15 THUR Sections row out in harbour for disembarkation practice. Get
... rose Aus. troopship Seang Chan tie up to shore, about 1,000 Aus
troops aboard former

16 FRI 6 boat crews of Rus. warship news
ashore march through Greek Ashold. 11 am Ruatine boy now
village ... French soldiers ...

17 SAT ... ... on board ... No 3 transport ... warship
... with aircraft guns & a sea ... arrive

The troopships arrive in Mudros harbour: disembarkation exercises.

A. BAYNE
(Bugler. 1st Bn. Wellington Regiment, N.Z.E.F.)

Lemnos, April 1915: a lunch break during trial landings.

R. L. Jones
(Pte. 11th Bn. A.I.F.)

Eve of the landings

Mudros harbour, Lemnos Island, was the point of final assembly for the great armada of vessels from which the combined operation would be launched. Here, on H.M.S. *London*'s quarterdeck, anti-mine nets are being prepared. Ahead lies the "Packet of Woodbines", the Russian cruiser *Askold*.

Cdr. G. Drage

probably leave him up in the top *[illegible]* without
food till he gets thin enough to drop
through the hole. Very interesting seeing
the whole ship from above the height
of the top of the funnels; the men were all
standing by the guns in case any land
batteries opened on us, and in the distance
we saw two battle ships and three destroyers
shelling some forts on shore and being
shelled in return; the land shooting was
very wild; the ships hit the land all
right, but as we couldn't see what they were
firing at I don't know whether they hit it.
Then we went into the same area, and we
were all hauled down into the casemates,

in deadly fear that they were going to
fire their colossal guns; luckily they
didn't. The Turks fired a few shots
from field-guns and one lot of three
shell from some sort of howitzer. I saw
one shell fall about a thousand yards
away and I don't think anything else was
much nearer. One felt pretty safe, as we
were loaded up with generals and admirals,
and they wouldn't risk the Turks making
a bag like that.

Well we are off in a day or two, if
the weather stays fine; just like the Greek
fleet going to Troy, people collected from
all over the known world; we have even
got our wooden horse which I will explain
later on. As far as the intelligence reports
tell us, however, there seems to be no Helen

The last letter written by an officer who was to earn a posthumous Victoria Cross on the day following the 25 April landing. This letter, dated 21 April from the troopship *Andania,* records that a number of officers had been taken by battleship to observe their objective. Captain Garth N. Walford, an officer in the Royal Artillery, was to be killed leading a storming party into the village and fort of Seddul Bahr above V beach.

CAPT. G. N. WALFORD V.C.

Each member of the 29th Division received a copy of this address which rather interestingly matches its inspirational intent with clear foreboding. Sir Ian Hamilton's force order also made reference to defences "vaunted by our enemies as impregnable" but declared that: "The landing will be made good, by the help of God and the Navy; the positions will be stormed, and the war brought one step nearer to a glorious close."

PERSONAL NOTE
FROM
MAJOR-GENERAL AYLMER HUNTER-WESTON, C.B., D.S.O.,
TO EACH MAN OF THE 29th DIVISION
ON THE OCCASION OF THEIR FIRST
GOING INTO ACTION TOGETHER.

The Major-General Commanding congratulates the Division on being selected for an enterprise the success of which will have a decisive effect on the War.

The eyes of the World are upon us and your deeds will live in history.

To us now is given an opportunity of avenging our friends and relatives who have fallen in France and Flanders. Our comrades there willingly gave their lives in thousands and tens of thousands for our King and Country, and by their glorious courage and dogged tenacity they defeated the invaders and broke the German offensive.

We also must be prepared to suffer hardships, privations, thirst, and heavy losses, by bullets, by shells, by mines, by drowning. But if each man feels, as is true, that on him individually, however small or however great his task, rests the success or failure of the Expedition, and therefore the honour of the Empire and the welfare of his own folk at home, we are certain to win through to a glorious victory.

In Nelson's time it was England, now it is the whole British Empire, which expects that each man of us will do his duty.

A. H-W.

To Corporal J. S. Griffin

from Aylmer Hunter-Weston

24 April: Australians about to leave a destroyer for the battleship H.M.S. *London*.

Capt. C. F. H. Churchill R.N.

24 April: Australians aboard H.M.S. *London en route* for the Gallipoli Peninsula.

Capt. C. F. H. Churchill R.N.

24 April: Australians aboard H.M.S. *London*.

Capt. C. F. H. Churchill R.N.

24 April: officers of the 9th Battalion Australian Imperial Force on board
H.M.S. *Prince of Wales*.

CDR. H. VETCH

25 April: the landing at "Anzac" Cove

41

Y.M.C.A. of Perth Western Australia
Field Service Department

The war boats had all stopped steaming, sailors were every where, moving about very silent, not a noise of any kind could be heard. The sea was as smooth as glass. The boats were being lowered into the water. The order came then to get into the boats. Every man was in a very short time seated in his respective boat, and and every thing was done in such a quiet manner that one would not realize that such a movement in the dark had been carried out. Each man had on his person a full pack consisting of one towel, one shirt, socks, great coat, cap, comforter, a change of under clothing, three sand bags rolled up and tied into the belt of the equipment at the back, Three days rations, consisting of from two to three tins preserved meat, three pounds of hard biscuits, and one emergency ration, consisting of ¼ of tea, two oz sugar & an extract of beef. They also had from two to three hundred rounds of ammunition. The boats were in four lines and a pinnace was in front of each line. They to tow us with in a certain distance from shore.

Y.M.C.A. of Perth Western Australia
Field Service Department

And then let us pull the rest of the way ourselves. Every thing was going well, and one can marvel at the way its was carried out for quietness. But an accident happened as we were nearing shore, one of the pinnaces' funnells caught fire, and sent up a flare that could be seen miles off. Then a voice rang out in the quietness, "You are going the wrong way, Bear over," but our man would not move out of his course, the voice rang out again, and then they tried to force us over by coming close alongside us. Still our man would not move out of his course so they towed us in, and made the landing in the place where our boat was making for. Now has it happened the place we landed at was wrong according to the place laid down. The correct place, being more to the right was covered with barbed wire. So the mistake was a God's send to every man that landed that Memorable morning. On nearing the shore the first thing that came to our notice was the flash of a huge search light, it appeared to come from cape Helles, and shortly afterward there came a second flash from farther round the cape

An account of the landing. The Australian and New Zealand Army Corps gave its initials as a name for the location which would be enshrined in the history of their respective countries. Later in 1915 a mortally wounded Australian gave these notes he had made of the Anzac landing to a private in a Medical Unit. The account goes on to state that there were orders laid down to: "fix bayonets and get into line, each man taking hold of the sleeve of the man next to him with his disengaged hand. But one can imagine to one's self why that was not carried out."

R. A. NICHOLAS
(Hospital Transport Corps.)

New Zealanders landing during the morning of 25 April at Anzac. The photographer took this picture as he himself had just reached the beach.

GEORGE MAY
(Sgt. 1st Bn. Auckland Regiment, N.Z.E.F.)

The Anzac terrain and the first ground to be stormed once the troops were off the beach.

Dr. W. E. Chadwick
(2nd Lt. 1/7 Essex)

As the first troops boldly stormed inland from the beach, they soon found that the unexpectedly rough broken terrain rendered all coordinated movement impossible. Battalions dissolved into separated groups of men, some making marvellous progress but without possibility of any support. It was this and the strengthening Turkish resistance which led to the disturbing lack of confidence by commanders, who felt that the men should be evacuated. Bringing a degree of organisation to the problem of supply, especially of water, were the engineers. Sapper G. C. Grove describes the beach on which he landed and the work he had to undertake.

G. C. GROVE
(2nd Field Company,
1st Australian Division)

others besides a number of destroyers. 4
We were towed ashore by a steam pinnace at about 6.45 A.m and landed under very heavy shrapnel fire with only one casualty. We got out of the boats knee deep into the sea and waded ashore. The 3rd infantry Brigade fixed bayonets in the water and in the face of a hot fire from rifles and maxim guns charged up the hill through the scrub. Poor old Billy Moore, Haddock's friend in No 1 Field Coy. was killed whilst getting ashore. Quite a number of sailors from the battleships and destroyers were killed and wounded. the beach was littered all over with bits of web equipment, bags of iron rations, caps, hats, rifles ammunition lying in amongst the dead and wounded. As a result of the charge the Turks at sight of the bayonet cleared for their lives and retired back over the hill on the beach, down the gully behind and up the next hill

and away over to the next where 5
they made a stand. They were then a mile away from the beach. They then opened fire with shrapnel and played the devil with our chaps who had to retire back to the next ridge nearer the beach they then began to entrench themselves. Meanwhile the number of wounded was terrible, the beach being simply choc-a-block with stretchers full of wounded. Packs and equipment had been left all over the place in the scrub and on the side of the gully. On our arrival we were ordered to proceed at once with stores up the gully behind the first ridge as near the firing line as possible and bore for water sufficient to keep the men in the trenches well supplied, besides the mules of the Indian Mountain Batteries and the machine guns. This we did and found a good spot in a sort of creek just behind the firing line

where there was a very fair stream
of water. This we dammed up, and sunk
a well behind out of this we obtained
quite a fair supply, ample to supply
the needs of all concerned. Troops on
the way to the firing line were stopping
all day to get a drink so we were
working pretty hard with the pumps
having to fall flat on the ground
every minute or so on account on
the shrapnel shells and bullets
bursting over and amongst us all the
time. There were a lot of snipers
about on the ridges so when passing
backwards and forwards to the beach
we had to keep under cover as much
as possible. Stretcher bearers and
A.M.C. passing unceasingly backwards
and forwards between the beach and
the firing line doing magnificent work.
Guard mounted over water reserve during
night. I had the 12 to 2 A.M. shift, very
dark when moon went down. Had to
keep our eyes very wide open in spite
of our tiredness. Did not get any real
all night on account of having to man

the pumps to supply the mules and
water carts with water. Wounded passing
all night. Heard that poor Capt. Bowick
of 6th Battalion had been killed soon after
landing. Indian Mountain Battery
took up a position during the night
on top of the ridge under which we
were working and at day-break opened
fire with shrapnel on the enemy's trenches
Monday April 26th 1915 -
4th Brigade landed without loss. We
are still keeping the Turks at bay, but
cries for reinforcements are almost
incessant. We want our artillery
very badly, as only one gun has been
landed and that only a field gun 18 pndr.
5 or 6 Turkish wounded brought in on
stretchers kicking up in a terrible wailing.
Our men sticking to it magnificently.
A sniper made an attack on one of our
stretcher bearers with a bill-hook. The
bearer however was too quick for him
and snatched the hook away from him
and nearly cut his head off with it.
Several German Officers killed and

25 April: Cape Helles, W beach

The two main landings at Cape Helles, where the Regular Army Division, the 29th, was to carry out the operations, were beaches at the very tip of the Peninsula, W and V beaches.

H.M.S. *Swiftsure* covering the W beach landing by bombarding Turkish defences. (Note the *River Clyde* in her grounded position at V beach — right of the photo.)

J. G. T. Taylor
(Surgeon R.N.V.R.)

3 — 1320 b. (Established— ?, 1900.) (Revised— February, 1914.)

NAVAL SIGNAL.

From— To—

P.O. of Watch—
Read by—
Reported by—
Passed by—
Logged by—
System—
Date— April 21st
Time— 4.30 – 5.30 am

round to get opposite "W" beach. Euryalus steered slowly but kept some way out as they expected to be shelled. Prince George did a lot of firing all this time at the cliffs including "W" beach but as it afterwards turned out she hadn't put them in the right place or at least not half enough of them. It was just getting daylight while this was going on and as it was misty it was very hard to see what "W" beach was like and where exactly it was. We had only rough maps of the place and as we approached it from a totally different direction to that

M. 1704/00
Sta. 6/14.

---

5 — 1320 b. (Established— ?, 1900.) (Revised— February, 1914.)

NAVAL SIGNAL.

From— To—

P.O. of Watch—
Read by—
Reported by—
Passed by—
Logged by—
System—
Date—
Time—

had not been properly shelled. They were pouring a terrific fire down on us and it is a most extraordinary thing how any of the cutters which were open and absolutely unprotected and crammed with men survived it. The soldiers had to jump out into about 3 feet of water and it was a most awful sight seeing them being shot down as soon as they got into the water and the wounded ones hanging on to the edge of the boats. Lots of slightly wounded men must have been drowned

M. 1704/00
Sta. 6/14.

S.— 1320 b. (Established— May, 1900.) (Revised— February, 1914.)

NAVAL SIGNAL.

From— To—

P.O. of Watch—
Read by—
Reported by—
Passed by—
Logged by—
System—
Date— April 25th
Time— 5.30 am

we expected you couldn't predict what sort of reception you were going to get. We slipped about 30 yds from the beach but my boat was close as we had come round the corner. We were nearly on the rocks and didn't only just stopped in time. All the tows slipped alright and pulled in without fouling each other. There were two rows of barbed wire the whole length of the beach. The Turks opened fire with maxims, pom-poms and rifles just as we slipped. You could see them standing up in their trenches which I obviously

M. 1704/00
Sta. 6/14.

1320 b. (Established— ?, 1900.) (Revised— February, 1914.)

NAVAL SIGNAL.

From— To—

P.O. of Watch—
Read by—
Reported by—
Passed by—
Logged by—
System—
Date— April 25th
Time— 6 am

When they got on to the beach they were held up by the barbed wire and got a terrible dose lot more casualties as the Turks practically mowed them down as they moved through the gaps in the wire which they had cut. The enemy's trenches had them to take the cliffs each side which were full of snipers and to rush about lots of trenches up the valley. The way they took the cliffs was splendid though of course they lost a lot of men while doing it. The Turks couldn't face a bayonet and as soon as some of them got to the top of the

M. 1704/00
Sta. 6/14.

The Lancashire Fusiliers at W beach: a midshipman of H.M.S. *Euryalus* uses official forms for his letter home describing the landing. On this tiny beach the Fusiliers suffered 533 casualties, of whom 189 were killed and 61 missing. Six Victoria Cross awards were earned.

CAPT. H. WILSON R.N.

W beach: the landing in progress.

CAPT. H. WILSON R.N.

Turkish prisoners from W beach aboard H.M.S. *Euryalus*.

CAPT. H. WILSON R.N.

27 April: a pontoon already in position at W beach to facilitate landing.

CAPT. H. WILSON R.N.

H. G. A. Knight of H.M.S. *Euryalus*: a painting of the W beach landing.

Midshipman A. M. Williams's steam pinnace. From H.M.S. *Euryalus* this boat assisted at the W beach landings.

Cdr. A. M. Williams

An aerial photo of W beach, renamed "Lancashire Landing", with its own pier for easier disembarkation.

'Grierson'
per Capt. E. F. Wettern (R.N.D.)

25 April: Cape Helles, V beach

At V beach, in addition to the tows of cutters and whalers brought in to the shore, an old collier, S. S. *River Clyde*, was run into the beach in order to disgorge safely the 2,000 troops in her holds. In fact there was a grim toll taken of the men, who had to rush from the exit points along the gangways leading to a lighter at *River Clyde*'s bows serving as a final bridge over the shallows. This photograph, taken by Dr. W. Harvey from the bows of *River Clyde*, provides crushing evidence of the failure of the naval bombardment to destroy the Turkish defensive positions. The lighter is filled with dead and wounded. Some troops having landed from the tows and from *River Clyde* are clustered together in the shelter of a low bank of shingle (see centre of photograph).

MAJOR W. G. HOLE

where the firing was much the hottest and after slipping the boats we went up alongside the port quarter of the Clyde bows away from the beach. Bullets were falling thick and fast and the beach itself was a regular death trap. The P.B. was struck several times and a bullet struck the side of the Clyde & my face was spattered with tiny nickel splinters. It missed my nose by an inch as I was standing up close to the Clyde. The two cutters in the tow pulled back from the beach with practically all their crews either killed or wounded. Forbes was in one & Mr Williams in the other. They went alongside the Clyde ahead of the P.B. Commander Diggle then came

back into the boat and just as he was standing on the top of the E.R. in front of the armour business a bullet got him in the knee. He sat down where he was and we took the cutters in tow and then lay off. Four more boats pulled off with most of their crews disabled and several soldiers lying wounded in them and these we also took in tow. Commander Diggle then directed us to proceed to the transport Arragon, but even with his wound he could not keep quiet cursing everyone in turn especially Barlow if he got the least bit off the course. As there is a 6 knot current running always off the straits it was jolly difficult to keep straight. His knee bled a good deal and

V beach: the crew of one of H.M.S. *Agamemnon's* picket boats witness tragedy and have their own problems.

CDR. H. BANKS

An aerial photo of V beach, Seddul Bahr village and castle with the *River Clyde* just to the left of the line of white wall and towers. Behind Seddul Bahr and to the right is the horseshoe shaped Morto Bay where the S beach landing took place. It was just off Morto Bay that the battleship H.M.S. *Goliath* was to be torpedoed by a Turkish surface vessel in May.

'GRIERSON'
per Capt. E. F. Wettern
(R.N.D.)

Men of the 2nd Battalion Hampshire Regiment or of the Dublin or Munster Fusiliers who fell in the attack on V beach.

J. BAREILLE
(Sgt. 4^{ieme} Rég Mixte Colonial)

The ruins of the village of Seddul Bahr.

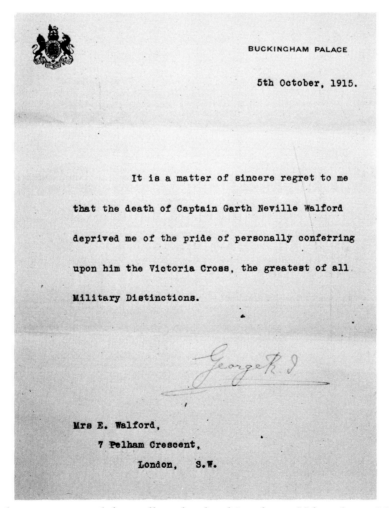

BUCKINGHAM PALACE

5th October, 1915.

It is a matter of sincere regret to me that the death of Captain Garth Neville Walford deprived me of the pride of personally conferring upon him the Victoria Cross, the greatest of all Military Distinctions.

George R.I.

Mrs E. Walford,
    7 Pelham Crescent,
        London, S.W.

A posthumous award for gallant leadership above V beach on 26 April when Captain Walford and two other officers rallied and led men to capture the village of Seddul Bahr.

Capt. G. N. Walford
(R.F.A.)

26 April: an unusual view of S.S. *River Clyde* run into the shingle of V beach.

Capt. H. Wilson R.N.

25 April: Cape Helles, X beach

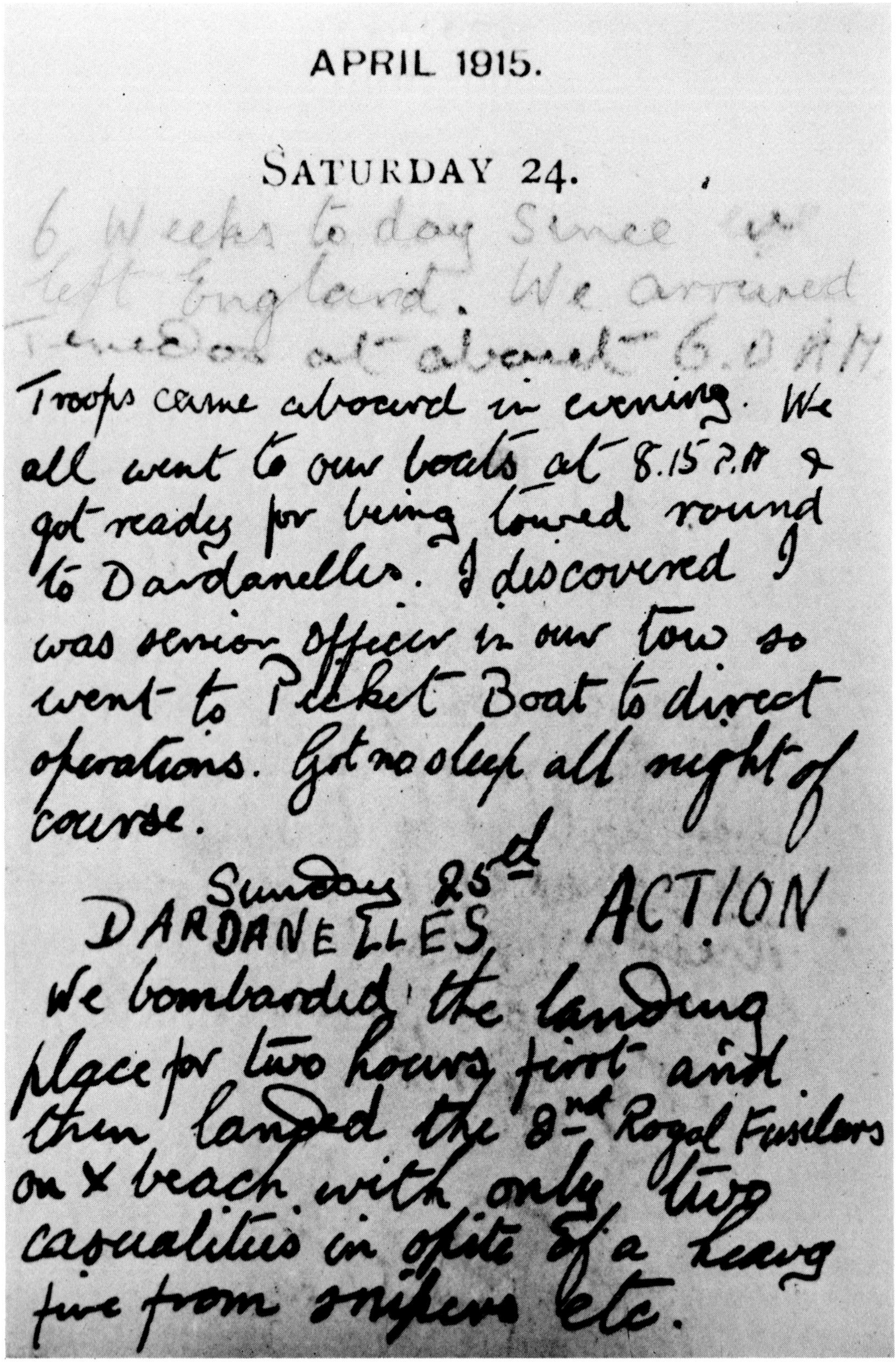

APRIL 1915.

SATURDAY 24.

6 Weeks to day since we left England. We arrived Tenedos at about 6.0 A.M. Troops came aboard in evening. We all went to our boats at 8.15 P.M & got ready for being towed round to Dardanelles. I discovered I was senior officer in our tow so went to Picket Boat to direct operations. Got no sleep all night of course.

Sunday 25d

DARDANELLES ACTION

We bombarded the landing place for two hours first and then landed the 2nd Royal Fusiliers on X beach with only two casualties in spite of a heavy fire from snipers etc.

Success at X beach, not least due to the skill with which H.M.S. *Implacable* was brought close in shore to shell the clifftop defensive emplacements. A midshipman's diary.

CDR. D. S. E. THOMPSON

25 April: X beach and its cliffs. The landing in progress.

Capt. H. Wilson R.N.

A track has now been cut into the cliffs of X beach.

A. M. Paterson
(R.E. attached to R.N.D.)

25/26 April: Cape Helles, Y beach

25 April: the French at Kum Kale

MONDAY 26.

Jack & I were called out at about two to go and fetch wounded from Y beach. This was the devil of a job to do in the dark. Our people are in an awful plight just got the beach they stand on & nearly run out of ammunition. There was a shower of bullets falling around us the whole time. Its much the most ticklish job I've had so far & I've had some stiff ones. I slept all the forenoon first time since Sat. morning. 4 boats have been sunk including ours so two crews can take a stand off we are doing so now as we have been in the thick of everything so far the other boats have gone to Y beach which is being evacuated. Fleet Surgeon was buried in afternoon. I was given A Chiens Picket Boat in evening.

TUESDAY 27.

Went away to X Beach in afternoon. Saw Tate again. Had Shells dropping around us for about 3 hours during forenoon. managed to secure one. Quite a decent job X. Beach nothing much of importance going on. 5000 Turks scotched.

A midshipman is called to take wounded from Y beach and then learns that this beachhead is to be evacuated. It had been taken quite easily on 25 April but no swift, supported advance inland had been made. Some clifftop perimeter defence had been dug, but the Turks, coming up in strength, were forcing the British to evacuate a position now scarcely tenable.

CDR. D. S. E. THOMPSON

French troops being towed in for the landing at Kum Kale on the Asiatic side of the entrance to the Dardanelles. This landing was designed to be temporary, its purpose being to appear to threaten these shores, thus keeping Turkish Asiatic stationed troops from swiftly assisting the defence of the Gallipoli Peninsula.

E. MALCAILLOZ
(Coporal 8^{ieme} Rég du Genie)

Cape Helles: the first attempt to take the village of Krithia

opened a terrific bombardment,
a terrible night. Monday 26/4/15 3.30 p.m. went out
to Inniskilling trenches & brought back
a wounded man who covered with
wounded, firing ceased about 4.30 p.m.
things quieter till evening when
the Turks began a fresh attack, got
a little sleep but was terribly cold
about the feet. A lovely day.
Tuesday 27/4/15
Made a small "dug out", brought
in more cases & attended to wounded
on the beach a rather slack day.
Wednesday 28/4/15
(Had a bathe.)
Spent the morning resting but
about 1.30 the wounded started
pouring in from the action a
general advance having been made.
about 2 p.m. went along the cliff to
assist the walking cases, got some back
in a rowing boat then brought in a
stretcher case over the land. made
another journey to an old farm used as an
aid post. volunteered to go to firing line
& bring in Major McBalister O.C. of K.O.S.B.
(firing had ceased) Shrapnel was burst
all about us. (He was wounded in right
pelvis & had to hold his leg all the way
Capt. gave morphia. brought in another
case after a little tea, got ringing wet
having put my jacket over wounded

A private in the 87th Brigade Field Ambulance (29th
Division) gives a diary account of tending to men wounded
in the attempt both to secure the beachhead gained and
advance upon the village of Krithia which stood at the foot
of the single dominant height called Achi Baba.

C. R. TOMKINSON

In the early days after the landing: wounded awaiting evacuation from X beach.

W. A. YOUNG
(87 Brigade Field Ambulance)

May: New Zealanders about to cross the deadly "Daisy Patch" at Cape Helles in the attack towards the village of Krithia. The photographer was to take shelter himself under the tree on the left and "bullets were cutting off the branches in good style".

GEORGE MAY
(Sgt. 1st Bn. Auckland Regiment, N.Z.E.F.)

Sitting pretty on one of the guns destroyed by naval shelling and then by landing party demolition at Cape Helles. A New Zealander's photo taken in May.

GEORGE MAY
(Sgt. 1st Bn. Auckland Regiment, N.Z.E.F.)

Gurkhas at Gurkha Bluff on the extreme left of the allied front line at Cape Helles.

W. A. YOUNG
(87th Brigade Field Ambulance)

24 May: the truce at Anzac

The blindfolded Turkish officer is in the Australian lines to negotiate a truce for the burial of the dead, after the slaughter of Turks in massed attacks on 19 May. There were also many dead who had lain unburied since a no man's land had been created by both sides having dug in so soon after the landing.

GEN. S. M. ANDERSON
(Australian Field Artillery)

The truce to clear no man's land.

GEN. S. M. ANDERSON

The truce to clear no man's land.

Gen. S. M. Anderson

by general Liman von Sanders and
Lt. Col. White one of our staff officers.
Seemed very queer all day with everything
so quiet no firing or anything all time.
Our men and Turks were exchanging
cigarettes and tobacco whilst some
were burying the dead. The smell was
something cruel most of the bodies
being almost totally decomposed.
The sight was most queer, men
sitting round in bunches smoking
and sharing their food with the
enemy, amidst dead bodies
amputated arms legs and heads
and general horrible surroundings.
Some of our chaps discovered that
one of the saps had got a bit out
of direction so, under cover of the
red cross flag would walk along,
suddenly stoop down as though,
to pick something up and then
stick a bayonet into the ground
to mark the correct line for the
trench to go. At about 3-45 or 40
PM our men were ordered back to

the trenches to be ready when the end
of the armistice came. At 4-30 as
punctual as possible shots were
exchanged between us and the
enemy. No very heavy firing was
experienced until 3·0 A.m. when the
Turks made a very faint hearted
attack which was easily repulsed
by our chaps without the loss of a
man on our side.

A diary account of the truce.

G. C. GROVE
(Sapper 2nd Field Company, 1st Australian Division)

The Anzac sector
day by day

Anzac Cove.

FRED ROGERS
(Sgt. 1st Bn. Otago Regiment, N.Z.E.F.)

A sniper caught.

A. M. PATERSON
(R.E. attached to R.N.D.)

Newly captured Turkish prisoner
being escorted down to the beach.

R. L. JONES
(Pte. 11th Bn. A.I.F.)

The path leading up to Quinn's Post.

G. May
(Sgt. 1st Bn. Auckland
Regiment, N.Z.E.F.)

Not much relief in a four-hour spell in reserve trenches below Quinn's Post. The post itself was at the top of a steep cliff and was reached by steps cut into the cliff. Separated dug out positions at the top were held in hand bombing combat over astonishingly short distances, even as little as seven yards. A New Zealander Cecil Malthus has written that "to lie cowering in the darkness of this cramped and evil smelling pit, and watch a big bomb sputtering among the corpses just against our lookhole, while waiting for the burst was an experience that no man could endure unmoved".

H. V. Palmer
(Pte. 1st Canterbury Bn., N.Z.E.F.)

June 22nd Tuesday
Left to relieve 1st Company at 8-30 A.M. I struck 2 relief giving us 4 hours off but could not sleep, our trouble in the trenches were if you laid down in the dust you got full of lice and annoyed by flies and men walking over you, when on duty was getting blown to pieces by bombs or the Turks tunnelling towards us and blowing in the trenches; mixed with a shower of dirt from machine gun and rifle fire from over head, but we were in a position to give them a little more back with trench mortors and hand grenades we had no casualties and left for another night rest

Orders issued from a dugout. The officer commanding B Squadron, Australian 5th Light Horse.

BRIG. J. G. McNEILL
(*Capt. 5th Light Horse*)

Private enterprise defeated. A Greek sailing ship attempts to land supplies at Watson's Pier, Anzac. She was shelled and stranded. Note the shell burst above the headland shown centre left.

BRIG. J. G. McNEILL

The dressing station on Plugge's Plateau. Colonel Plugge is in the centre.

G. May
(Sgt. 1st Auckland Regiment, N.Z.E.F.)

A relief force filing up from Brown's Dip to Lone Pine.

Brig. J. G. McNeill

An 18 pounder field gun dug in at Anzac.

R. L. Jones
(Pte. 11th Bn. A.I.F.)

Surprise encounter! Sir Ian Hamilton in an Anzac trench.

BRIG. J. G. MCNEILL

Open air barber: Anzac.

DR. W. E. CHADWICK
(2nd Lt. 1/7 Essex)

An Anzac mealtime for those not in the line.

A. E. ROBINSON
(Pte. 1st Bn. Auckland Regiment, N.Z.E.F.)

"Monash", or "Shrapnel" Gully looking towards the sea.

A. E. ROBINSON
(Pte. 1st Bn. Auckland Regiment, N.Z.E.F.)

The dugouts of Pope's Hill photographed from a gun position on Walker's Ridge.

A. E. ROBINSON
(Pte. 1st Bn. Auckland Regiment, N.Z.E.F.)

Mules under fire: the commanding officer of the Indian Army Mule Corps unit at Anzac has decisions to make over the rescue of his mules. In this diary there is evidence of very close unit comradeship, but at the same time there was stern discipline. In July, after court martial, an Indian was sentenced to 30 lashes after he had been caught thieving from the beach. In the superintended flogging: "The prisoner howled from the beginning. A trumpeter of 26 Mountain Battery flogged him very well."

LT. COL. H. M. ALEXANDER

New Zealanders Hope and McGregor stand behind S. Samuels delousing his shirt.

F. ROGERS
(Sgt. 1st Otago Battalion N.Z.E.F.)

Delousing: first the shirt and then the trousers.

DR. W. E. CHADWICK
(2nd Lt. 1/7 Essex)

The Australian 5th Light Horse in the trenches.

Brig. J. G. McNeill
(Capt. 5th Light Horse)

Front line New Zealand held trench at Anzac. The bayonets protruding from the ground are carrying the field telephone lines.

R. Howard

My impressions of the behaviour of our troops.

Slinging off and jeering at officers.

Have seen niggers beaten for oranges & chocolate, because they would not bring prices down.

The niggers beat them right & left when they loaded, now they pinch & upset stuff & bomb about it.

In the heart Ali mosque there are lads who enter with their hats on. Also break the glass & take it from the great lamp overhead. They have no idea of sacredness in regard to fine buildings.

A lot of them are very pig headed with regard to fares on the trams.

No respect for N.C.O's men simply ignore them.

Born grumblers & growl at everything. Living on the land & tucker: yet if they have to wait for pay then.

No idea of playing the game.

The way the Aust are tormented whether in tram cars. Restaurant. Walking in the streets. Backsheesh; clean boots. Postcard: also at the pyramids, the guides are very persistent. Australia very good: Plenty money.

Always referring to get out of jobs & going back yet when pay is late, what a shindy.

The ways they tormented niggers when they were loading goods into our ships.

Economical measures are never practised by our boys; when things are about. Peninsula issue?

Also the food that was pinched on the beach.

Chafingerers; Cold feet; Cannot behave; Schlenker; Peninsula accidents; Continuing Tommies in action: yet some of our lads were found wanting.

An Australian looks at Australians. Opinions expressed in a 1915/16 diary by Sapper G. C. Grove, 2nd Field Company 1st Australian Division.

These six photographs are from the unlabelled glass slides of Stuart M. Anderson, the officer in command of the Australian artillery at Anzac.

GEN. S. M. ANDERSON

4 June: battling for Krithia

One of the major Anglo-French frontal assaults of May, June and July at Cape Helles took place on 4 June. Though some deception was used in delaying the attack, when the preliminary bombardment was halted momentarily and then resumed to catch the Turks manning the firestep of their trenches, no significant allied gains were made. In a letter of 11 June, a British officer of the 14th Sikhs, who had led his men into action on 4 June, considered that "bald-headed" tactics had been employed. The officer himself was incorrectly reported as killed, his parents having their sorrow lifted a few days after receiving official notification of their son's death. Another Indian Army officer (6th Gurkhas), but one who was serving at Anzac, recorded Australian officers as "a very nice set of men and most of them are absolute Sahibs".

LT. GEN. SIR REGINALD SAVORY

1/10th M.R.   June 4th/15
Med: Exp: Force

My dear Mother
    Just a line to let you
know I am still very fit.
I know you will be always
anxious for news. That is
why I just send a scrap.
I really have no time for
more, as we are frightfully
busy now, digging day
and night. I am a
qualified navvy & Engineer
now. We are still attached
to the Royal Fusiliers, and
are getting on very well.
My best love to all &
thanks for letters dated
May 13th. Your loving son
            H. K. B. Nevinson

A last letter written on the morning of the attack on Krithia in which the writer was to be mortally wounded. He gave the letter to the corporal who attempted to aid him.

2ND LT. H. K. B. NEVINSON
1/10 Manchesters

Sept 1915
77, Webster St
Oldham

To

Mr & Mrs Nevinson

I will just write you a few lines and explain how
our dear Officer and your son met his end perhaps you have
forgotten with the sudden shock, and hoping I am not doing
wrong in repeating it. On June 4th at 11.20 A.M. we are
going to take two Turkish trenches. Our artillery put
5,000 shells in the turkish trenches this occupying ten
minutes, then we put our bayonets over the trenches and
cheer as if about to charge this brings the turks from the
second line to the front line, then our artillery put 19000
shells in the turks front line. It does not look as if their
could be a turk left alive. Now every other man must
charge the turks front line and the remainder to charge
through them and take the second line. this was accomplished
although we lost half our Batt. in one hour. Our Lieut
must have jumped out to lead his men as I know he
would do and he was shot in the right groin. the bullet
I heard later piecered his bladder, I found him in the
trench with a lot of dead and wounded. I cleared the trench
of the dead and then made the remainder warm with
blankets. Mr Nevinson spoke to me and smiled but never
thought about dying. He looked so pretty when I covered him
up and I loved him so much that I had to kiss him. He

Part 2

just looked a little boy. He gave me a note to
go to the beach on duty. this being the last note he
wrote you whould like to have it for a keep sake I
know and I also send you a photo of myself in Scout
Uniform that was taken in 1911. On June 12th 1911 I
arrived at London with a dispatch from Oldham a distance
of 200 Miles, I passed through Market Harborough and
Leicter. North Hampton.

The dispatch was to Baden Powell
and I completed the journey in 3½ days
walking all the way.

truly yr. Cpl
Wm Parker

The corporal writes to the parents of 2nd Lieutenant Nevinson whom he
had found mortally wounded during the battle of 4 June at Helles.

H. K. B. NEVINSON papers

a bit. I don't mind, as it is a change, & I really was getting fed up with wielding, the shove and pickel all the time.

"Asiatic Annie" is trying to give us socks again & has plonked about eight big uns round about since I started this letter. Isn't it annoying? On a Sunday evening too! We get into the way of looking at these little disturbances in much the same light as you regard the organ grinder, in the lane who starts up just when you are helping Jeff find the mistake in the trial balance.

I see that some of our little advances are mentioned in the papers, tho' they don't exactly mention us in despatches. We were to have been in the big do on June 4th, and to have followed up behind the attacking line and got the captured trenches in a state of defence. And we should have known all about it too! As it was, we got up to our own front line (after waiting in rear whilst the bombardment was on) just as the retirement

from the captured trenches was ordered, so could only stand & watch our chaps coming back over the parapet — those that could get back, that is. It was a rotten disappointment, right. We waited about there all day, but there was nothing further doing, except that our artillery gave the lost trenches what for again in the afternoon — just for spite, I suppose. I was watching them closely, & it looked as if they were being blown half-way to Constant.

The last few weeks we have spent in sapping, mainly in front of our lines. It is a funny job, & you don't want to put your head out and admire the scenery. It is apt to be exciting, especially at night & if there happen to be any Turks messing around with bombs. It is also very monotonous — barring the bomb part of it. A Turkish gentleman came over the top of one of our saps one dark night. He gave our chaps a bit of a shock, as they didn't know whether the

Being shelled and "on a Sunday evening too". The characteristic humour and understatement of this letter writer are stretched in describing the events of 4 June. The final sentence continues overleaf: "the rest of the Turkish army was coming too, and wondered whether they should stay and see".

CAPT. E. F. WETTERN
(Sapper. R.N.D. Engineers)

went into reserve trenches under shrapnel fire all evening. Just left one spot about two minutes before a shell burst, posted to C Company. Shared dug out with Emerton. Heavy rifle fire at midnight.

2.6.15 Received orders from company commander Capt. Harman, Capt. Gilbert 2nd in command. Took over command of No 10 Platoon with Lieut. Spragg T. supernumerary. Took up dug-out in centre of Platoon with Pte Hoon as servant. Bathing.

3.6.15 In same dug-outs inspections bathing

4.6.15 Big advance ordered. Strong points bombarded between 8 & 10.30 am. 100 m. moved into support trenches under heavy shell fire. Lieut Spragg killed by shrapnel. Hit in the head & heart. Moved along support trenches during our heavy artillery bombardment. Platoon Sergeant Carlin and many others wounded. Arrived in first line trenches ordered by Capt. Gilbert to advance over

the parapet with my platoon, this I did under a very heavy rifle and machine gun fire and lay down about ten yards out. One man hit on my right through the chin getting down, he managed to crawl back to the trench. I found the man on my left was dead. After waiting here for about twenty minutes unable to get in touch with anyone on either flank and having only five men left I decided to crawl back to the trench and jump in. This we did and received a message to reform the company to support the Gurkhas. Found Garrood had been wounded in advancing over the parapet. In the evening we moved into trenches to support the L.Y.

5.6.15 Kept in support trenches until relieved by at 5 p.m. Returned old dug outs moved about 10 p.m. leaving E. Lanes T who had been attached to us

An officer from the Royal Warwicks attached to the 1st Battalion Royal Inniskilling Fusiliers advances ten yards with his platoon, then with "only five left I decided to crawl back to the trench and jump in".

LT. COL. J. HAIGH

Helles: day by day with the Royal Naval Division on the right of the line

Royal Naval Division sappers relax in Morto Bay: de Tott's Battery in the rear, somewhere to the right "Asiatic Annie", the gun which from across the Narrows maintained an irregular fire on the British held beaches at Cape Helles.

'GRIERSON'
PER CAPT. E. F. WETTERN
(Sapper. R.N.D. Engineers)

Sir Ian Hamilton visits the Royal Naval Division sector at Cape Helles.

CAPT. E. F. WETTERN

A medical unit shows support for its doctor: the legs belong to Surgeon Mayne.

DR. C. MAYNE *(R.N.D.)*

Two 60 pounder guns at Cape Helles.

A. M. PATERSON
(R.E. attached to R.N.D.)

W beach becoming a base area but always within shell fire.

A. M. PATERSON
(R.E. attached to R.N.D.)

Catching frogs in Krithia Nullah. (French sector in near vicinity!)

CAPT. E. F. WETTERN

Catapult in action: R.N.D. engineers at Cape Helles.

CAPT. E. F. WETTERN

A dry gully widened as cover for horses, Cape Helles.

A. M. PATERSON
(R.E. attached to R.N.D.)

Mulish behaviour at a Royal Naval Division dump in "Eastern Mule Trench". Note the drums of barbed wire (left foreground).

'GRIERSON'
PER CAPT. E. F. WETTERN

The photographer captures his feet in trenches being dug at Helles.

W. ASTLEY
(R.N.D. Engineers)

Skew Bridge under construction.

CAPT. E. F. WETTERN

Romano's Well and its drinking trough.

CAPT. E. F. WETTERN

The White House.

CAPT. E. F. WETTERN

Backhouse Post and Krithia Nullah.

Capt. E. F. Wettern

Fir Tree Copse.

Capt. E. F. Wettern

The expertise of an R.N.D. engineer sign writer.

Capt. E. F. Wettern

Aerial support: the Royal Naval Air Service on the island of Imbros

Apart from seaplanes from the seaplane carriers, land based planes from the island of Imbros supported the military operations. An aeroplane packing case provided accommodation for Number 3 Wing officers on the island. Pin-up pictures helped to give the interior a more attractive look. (No doubt the Bournville chocolate biscuit tins had long lost their original contents in the Mediterranean climate.)

SQUADRON LEADER H. A. BUSS

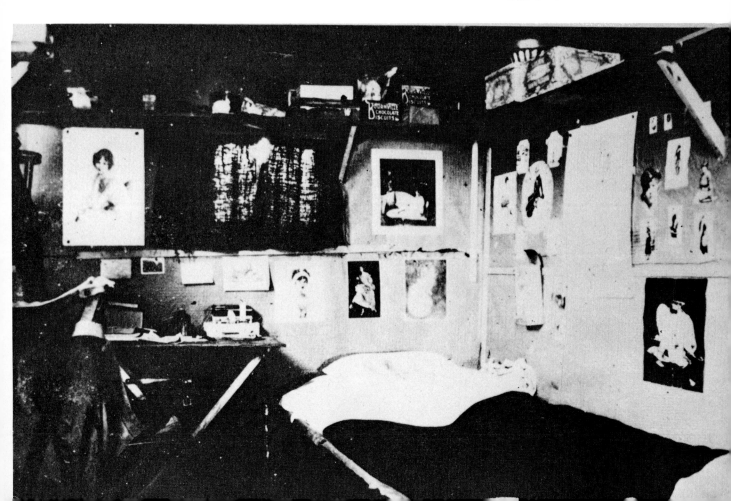

Cameras used in aerial photography over the Dardanelles: Number 2 Wing, island of Imbros.

W. M. GARNER

The graves of R.N.A.S. flying personnel from Number 3 Wing, Island of Imbros. The grave of C. H. Collet, a captain in the Royal Marine Artillery and at the same time an R.N.A.S. flight commander, is on the left. He had been burned to death in a crash after engine failure.

W. M. GARNER

Successfully attacked a merchant ship off Gallipoli.
This is the initial effort in the Torpedo carrying line + ought to
bear fruit. Edmonds did awfully well, flying at 1500 feet only
over the Bulair lines, he made his attack about 700 yds away
within 15 feet of the water.
A submarine attacked + missed H.M.S. Manica off Suvla this
forenoon - this is the re-appearance of "Fritz". Bad luck to him.

August 19th 1915. We have had no news whatever from
the Army since the commencement of operations, + therefore
take a dismal view of the situation. We are in for
a long tedious winter campaign.
The enemy Submarines have been active but ineffective.
except in the case of the Royal George or Edward (?)
which was sunk in the Aegean with the loss of
900 men.
The last few days have been unlucky ones for Aviation.
Three of our good machines (136, 161 + 762) have done in
their under-carriages + Cmdr Samson' squadron landed
frightfully bad luck. Yesterday a Voisin was done in
+ today Ft. Cmdr Collet was killed in a B.E.
He left the aerodrome to take spare engine parts to
the Commander, who had landed at Suvla, + when
at 150 feet his engine failed. The wind was strong +
the gusts very bad over the Kephalo cliff +, when
making a turn to land again, he lost control of the
machine + came to earth with a fearful crash, as the
result of a nose dive + side slip. The machine caught
fire before the Pilot could be rescued he had been
burnt beyond recognition. Death resulted half an
hour afterwards. His passenger, an E.R.A, broke his
thigh + suffered from severe burns (these trying to
rescue his Officer).
Collet's loss is indeed a serious one. A keen +
clever Soldier, an equally keen + efficient Aviator
+ his charming + quiet demeanour endeared him to all

An R.N.A.S. seaplane pilot records the first successful aerial torpedo attack in history, but recognises that the August offensive at Suvla is making no progress. Geoffrey Bromet also relates the grim details of the fatal air crash of Flight Commander Collet on the island of Imbros.

AIR VICE MARSHAL SIR G. R. BROMET

The Navy after the April landings

Apart from the superb submarine achievements, the Navy adopted a secondary and supportive role to the Army from the end of April. This role, vital though it was, became further curtailed after the loss of three old battleships in May, but nevertheless the Army was in a real sense totally dependent on the Navy and not merely for its eventual evacuation! Here in the foreground is the old battleship H.M.S. *Majestic*. More distant is the new 15 inch gun dreadnought battleship H.M.S. *Queen Elizabeth* . On 27 May *Majestic* was to be torpedoed and to sink off W beach, her keel for some time remaining above the water.

W. A. YOUNG

The German crew of the *Muavenet* which torpedoed the battleship H.M.S. *Goliath* in Morto Bay on the night of 12/13 May. Over 600 British officers and ratings were lost from *Goliath*.

22 May: H.M.S. *Canopus* attempts to haul the grounded H.M.S. *Albion* from potential disaster at Gaba Tepe. Destroyers assisted too in the successful work to free *Albion*. All this was done under heavy fire; little wonder that a midshipman concerned in the affair wrote to his mother confessing that he was now smoking but "in moderation . . . it is very soothing".

CAPT. L. A. K. BOSWELL
(A midshipman but not the self-confessed smoker.)

at 12-7 P.m. we saw the shell of a submarine appear out of the water almost immediately there was a splash, a report and then to our alarm and disgust a terific explosion occurred on board the H.M.S. Triumph at once, a column of water shot up into the air as high as the mastheads she listed to starboard almost immediately and gradually began to lean over more and more. I at once got my telescope on her and could see the sailors all lining the decks. A large puff of black smoke came from the funnels and then everything was clear and we knew the fires had been drawn to avoid an explosion. Already destroyers were hurrying at full speed to the scene. From the beach could be heard the order "4 steam pinnaces make at full speed for Triumph. Within a few minutes they were there

her side and turned turtle, her propellors being seen easily sticking up clear of the water. Through the telescope men could be seen floating in the water, climbing up onto the pinnaces and destroyers and lining the decks of the latter. Within a few minutes other destroyers were racing off in all directions to search for the submarine. One destroyer fired 4 shots at something in the water but it could not be seen whether they had hit anything or not. At 12-19 the Triumph sank below the water having taken 12 minutes from the time she was hit until the time she disappeared at about 12-30 P.m. Left dressing station and was sent on board H.M.S. "Newmarket" fleet sweeper at 7-30 P.m. after having been in casualty clearing hospital for about 4 hours. We left the beach in a lighter towed by a picket boat and were transfered

25 May. The first of U21's victims:
The torpedoing of H.M.S. *Triumph* closely observed from Anzac. Two days later U21 found further battleship prey, H.M.S. *Majestic*, off Cape Helles.

G. C. GROVE
(Sapper. 2nd Field Company,
1st Australian Division)

A safe retreat from U boats: Mudros Harbour in June. Foreground left to right: H.M.S. *Prince George*, H.M.S. *Cornwallis*, S.S. *Olympic* (troopship). Centre rear S. S. *Mauretania* (troopship).

J. G. T. TAYLOR
(Surgeon R.N.V.R.)

The Australian submarine AE2 photographed in the Suez Canal. She was the first allied submarine to force her way into the Sea of Marmara but four days after this achievement she was to be lost in action with Turkish warships, (30 April) her crew being taken prisoner.

W. T. HENSON
(Chief Petty Officer: H.M.S. Agamemnon)

The viaduct at Eski Hissar photographed in 1972. This viaduct was blown up in 1915 in a daring land enterprise from the British submarine E11. The spectacular nature of this achievement, (even exceeded by the successful sinking of Turkish vessels actually in waters off Constantinople,) should not conceal the utility of the prolonged stranglehold exerted on Turkish waterborne military supplies to their troops on the Peninsula. Every time a submarine broke through the net defences at the Narrows she had still to face dangers from mines, surface vessels, shore batteries, aeroplanes and searchlight location at night when necessarily on the surface for recharging the batteries to work the dynamos for undersea travel, yet in August, E11 in a 29 day cruise bagged not merely the viaduct but a battleship, a gunboat, six transports, an armed steamer and twenty-three sailing vessels.

till 9.20 when we dived and searched another of their harbours. At 1.30 got bow tube ready to fire at steamer but found she was already ashore so let her off. Saw a small dhow so went over alongside her, rose till our conning tower was out of water and put our prisoners aboard her. Dived straight away out of it. Expect the Turks in dhow had a fright when we appeared alongside. Carried on diving till 4.30. Came up started engines and charged batteries till 9.0. Went down then for the night. Monday. 6th came up

at 4.15 A.M. and made our way over to the islands which we had not visited for a few days. They must have got bold as they had not seen us lately for we got our best bag of any day up there. At 8.15 we sighted several dhows and sank 5 of them by gun fire. Between 9 and 10 sunk one large dhow by gun fire and rammed another. Proceeded and at 11.50 caught and rammed another. At 12.5 sunk one by ramming and burnt another. At 1.40 started firing at a bunch of six dhows lying off the shore and finished

The exploits of one of our submarines operating in the Sea of Marmara and off Constantinople.

THE DIARY OF PETTY OFFICER STEPHENS OF E2.

them off by 3 o'clock. After that we started firing at several more lying off shore but as they gave us back rifle fire from the shore too very hot and it was getting dusk we cleared out. Altogether had a very good day, sunk and otherwise destroyed 16 dhows and got rid of 122 rounds of ammunition. Charged and at 8.50 went down to 60 ft for the night. On 7th called hands at 3.15 and proceeded under water till 6.30 when we came to surface and had a look round. Nothing doing so went down again.

Came up at 7.40 and proceeded under engines towards Constantinople. Picked up a dhow on the way and burnt her. Charged battery right up and at 4.55 dived towards the shore sticking our nose into the beach at 60 ft about 8.30 and settled down for the night. Prepared a gun cotton charge for our first lieutenant to take ashore in an endeavour to damage the railway. We got on the move at 2 A.M and made our way nearer in shore till we reached 20 ft. First lieutenant went off with his charge about 3 A.M. Since then we havn't seen him.

The French at Cape Helles

Contemplation and co-operation. French soldiers and S.S. *River Clyde*. From 27 April the French forces landed at Kum Kale were transferred to Cape Helles. Here they held the extreme right of the line which was established across the tip of the Peninsula as the opposing forces dug in and launched costly frontal assaults in which the French on several occasions suffered severe casualties.

H. TOURNEBISE
(Radio Telégraphiste)

Wounded Senegalese aboard the *St. Helena* evacuating them to Mudros after the 3rd Battle of Krithia on 4 June.

DR. F. BEURIER
(Medical officer)

Wounded French soldiers in a Field Hospital on the island of Lemnos.

R. HOWARD

Dr. Baus, Medical Officer for the Senegalese troops. His "Chien Sanitaire" looks attendantly alert.

DR. F. BEURIER

Senegalese troops relaxed but in the trenches.

J. Bareille

The conferring of decorations "in the field". A French gunner receives the Croix de Guerre.

J. Bareille

French firing a heavy gun from Seddul Bahr.

J. Bareille

French infantry of the 176th Regiment.

C. Thierry
(Caporal 176^{ieme} Rég d'Infanterie)

Burial of a French doctor, Dr. Chassè, six French officers having been killed on the same day.

Dr. E. Beurier

On the line as well as in it! French field telephone in operation at an ammunition supply point.

Commandant R. Weil
(Lieutenant 8ieme Rég d'Artillerie)

French gun battery position being protected at Eski Hissarlik, Cape Helles, in May.

Commandant R. Weil

The famous French 75 mm guns in action. 32 Battery of the 8th Artillery Regiment in action at Eski Hissarlik in June.

Commandant R. Weil

May: a forward artillery observation post. The officer in command of a gun battery searches for his targets.

Commandant R. Weil

A miscellany of humour and sadness, the ordinary and extraordinary

"They were only playing leapfrog": respite in relaxation.

DR. W. E. CHADWICK
(2nd Lt. 1/7 Essex)

Cape Helles dispatch rider. Surely his route was seldom as uncluttered as this!

A. M. PATERSON
(R.E. attached to R.N.D.)

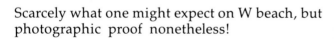

Scarcely what one might expect on W beach, but photographic proof nonetheless!

A. M. PATERSON
(R.E. attached to R.N.D)

PENINSULA PRESS.

No. 41   WEDNESDAY, JUNE 30th 1915.   Official News.

Gaining Ground in the Peninsula.

The plan of operations on Monday was to throw forward the left of our line South-east of Krithia, pivoting on a point about one mile from the sea, and, after advancing the extreme left for about half a mile, to establish a new line facing East on ground thus gained.

This plan entailed the capture in succession of two lines of Turkish trenches East of the Saghir Dere and five lines of trenches West of it. The Australian Corps was ordered to co-operate by making a vigourous demonstration. The action opened at 9 a.m. with the bombardment, by heavy artillery of the trenches to be captured. The assistance rendered by the French in this bombardment was most valuable. At 10.20 our Field Artillery opened fire to cut the wire in front of the Turkish trenches and this was effectively done. Great effect on enemy's trenches near the sea and in keeping down his artillery fire from that quarter was produced by the very accurate fire of H.M.S. "Talbot," "Scorpion" and "Wolverine." At 10.45 a small Turkish advanced work in the Saghir Dere, known as the Boomerang redoubt, was assaulted. This little fort was very strongly sited, protected by extra strong wire entanglements and has long been a source of trouble.

After special bombardment by French mortar, and while the bombardment of surrounding trenches was at its height, part of the Border Regiment, at the exact moment prescribed, leapt from their trenches as one man, like a pack of hounds streaming out of cover, raced across and took the work most brilliantly. The artillery bombardment increased in intensity till 11 a.m. when the range was lengthened and the infantry advanced.

The infantry attack was carried out with great dash along the whole line. West of Saghir Dere the 87th Brigade captured three lines of trenches with little opposition. The trenches were full of dead Turks, many buried by the bombardment, and one hundred prisoners were taken in them. East of the ravine two battalions of Royal Scots made a fine attack, capturing the two lines of trenches assigned as their objective, but the remainder of the 156th Brigade on their right met with a severe opposition and were unable to get forward.

At 11.30, the 86th Brigade, led by 2nd Royal Fusiliers, started the second phase of attack West of the ravine. They advanced with great steadiness and resolution through the trenches already captured, and on across the open, and taking two more lines of trenches reached the objective allotted to them, the Lancashire Fusiliers inclining half-right and forming line to connect with our new position East of the ravine.

The northernmost objective had now been attained, but the Gurkhas pressing on under the cliffs captured an important knoll still further forward, actually due West of Krithia. This they fortified and held during the night making our total gain on the left of precisely one thousand yards. During the afternoon the 88th Brigade attacked a trench, a small portion of which remained uncaptured on the right, but the enemy held on stubbornly, supported by machine guns and artillery and the attacks did not succeed.

During the night the enemy counter-attacked the furthest trenches gained but was repulsed with heavy loss. A party of Turks who penetrated from the flank between the two lines of captured trenches, were subjected to machine gun fire at daybreak, suffered very heavily and survivors surrendered. Except for a small portion of the trench already mentioned, which is still held by the enemy, all and more than was hoped for from the operation has been gained. On the extreme left our line has been pushed forward to a specially strong point well beyond the limit of the advance originally contemplated. The line gained is being consolidated and is much more advantageously sited than that previously held. The enemy's casualties are reported to be very severe. Our casualties were about 2,000, the greater proportion of which are slight cases of which 250 were at Anzac in the useful demonstration made simultaneously there.

All engaged did well but certainly the chief factor in the success was the splendid attack carried out by 29th Division whose conduct in this, as on previous occasions, was beyond praise.

Quiet on the Western Front.

Paris, 29th

The official report issued last evening says:—
Along the whole front the day was comparatively quiet. North of Souchez, at Neuville and Rochincourt, there was an artillery duel. Arras has again been bombarded with heavy guns. Between the Oise and the Aisne artillery engagements are proceeding in favour of the French. In the Argonne and on the heights of the Meuse, along the trench of Calonne, the Germans have not renewed their attack after the check of last night.
During the morning of the 27th a French airman succeeded in throwing five bombs on the Zeppelin sheds of Friedrichshaffen. His motor failed and during the return journey he had to come down at Rheinfezden, in Swiss territory.

To Repeat the Crime of Rheims.

Not content with destroying historic buildings at Rheims, Louvain and Arras, the German Vandals are casting malicious eyes on St. Mark's, Venice, and on Milan Cathedral. The "Vossische Zeitung" has already made the discovery that wireless telegraphic apparatus and anti-aircraft guns have been placed on these famous churches, and that the Austrians would be justified in making air attacks on them.
The Austrians were not slow to take the hint. One of their aeroplanes aimed a bomb at St. Mark's. Luckily, it fell in the Royal Garden a few yards from St. Mark's Square.
(Egyptian Gazette).

City Men as War Workers.

The authorities at the Royal Arsenal, Woolwich, have accepted the offer of a number of city business men to devote their Sundays to helping in the manufacture of munitions. A similar offer has been made by salesman of Smithfield. The work allotted to these amateur munition makers will, of course, be of a simple, though not less valuable, character, and, as time goes on, each will be given the duties for which he proves best fitted. Each man will be paid at the standard rates for the work he is doing. (London Paper).

R.E. Printing Section, G.H.Q., M.E.F.

On the back of one of these Mediterranean Expeditionary Force news-sheets a soldier has written: "We don't get the bad news. This is the only source of information." The news-sheet reports the attack on 28 June. Lines of Turkish trenches were captured but at a fearsomely worse cost than is reported here.

LOST.

A German submarine. Anybody returning same to K. Bill will be rewarded.

LITERARY SUPPLEMENT.

"Y" BEACH.

"Y" Beach, the Scottish Borderer cried
While panting up the steep hillside,
               "Y" Beach!
To call this thing a beach is stiff,
It's nothing but a b—— cliff.
            Why beach?

THE BLUE OF THE ÆGEAN.

How blue is the sea at Hissarlik,
How blue is the water at "V,"
How blue is the sky in the heavens,
And how lovely the "W" sea.

ODE TO TENEDOS.

O Tenedos, thy peaceful island green
A stirring passage in the fight has seen;
Eight generals and half-a-hundred men
First packed their kit, and then unpacked again.

CORRESPONDENCE.

Sir,—As a strict grammarian my ear is offended by the prevalent system of referring to officers, recalled for service during the war, as "Dug Outs." May I suggest that this form of the plural is strictly ungrammatical, and that the name should be spelt "Dugs Out."

           Yours etc.,
               PETER PAN.

AMPHITHEATRE ROYAL

"V" Beach.

Twice daily.   Twice daily.

A Screaming Farce entitled

"ANNIE from ASIA."

ADVERTISEMENTS

ANZAC!   ANZAC!!   ANZAC!!!
The Great Stickfast!

Liman von Sanders writes:—
  "It's glutinous powers exceeded all my expectations."

Enver Pasha writes:—
  "The bottle you kindly sent me suffices all my needs. I do **not** want any more. I find a little goes a long way."

NO ARMY SHOULD BE WITHOUT IT.

Try it To-day.
ANZAC!   ANZAC!

HARROD'S HAT STRETCHERS

Specially recommended for the Staff.
    Price 10s. 6d.   Post Free 11s.

HOLIDAY REMOVALS!

Carefully executed by Camp Commandant & Co.
Any quantity catered for.
DON'T STINT YOURSELVES!
No extra charge up to any amount.
Weight no object.
Special arrangements for guides and detectives.
Work for all inhabitants.
Come as often as possible.
We pack and unpack simultaneously.
No changes of mind, locality, and kits are neglected.
The Greek Governor of Tenedos signals:—
  Now I have seen your arrangements I know Constantinople must fall.
An Officer writes:—
  "Where the ——— is my valise."

RACING INTELLIGENCE.

          Tenedos, May 16th.
10 p.m. Grub Street Stakes.
"Dardanelles Driveller" (by G.S.—Imagination) m. Braithwaite junr . . . 1.
Also ran: "P.P." (by Reuter—Yes I dont think) aged, Maxwell . . . . . . fell.
  P.P. jumped off with the start, but never looked like a winner, and fell at the third fence, Dardanelles Driveller finishing alone.
  Winner trained by Winchester.
  P.P. looks a likely horse for the stud

The Dardanelles Driveller for 17 May: a short lived humorous trench news-sheet.

LT. COL. H. M. ALEXANDER

The puckish label with this sketch from either
Imbros or Mudros reads: "Wives of a Turkish
soldier applying for separation allowances."

CAPT. E. F. WETTERN

Peninsula humour.

T. W. WALKER

Gallipoli
August 5. 1915

Dear Mother,

Little enough did I think 12 months ago to-day that on the anniversary of mobilisation I should be writing you from a hole in the Gallipoli Peninsular, not having seen you for 10½ months, and to the tune of 75ᵐᵐ guns. However you never know your luck, and I may see you in time to celebrate my 20ᵗʰ birthday at home, tho' as things look at present, there's not much chance of that.

I have received 2 letters from you, July 8ᵗʰ & 13ᵗʰ. Also Auntie Ada's ———— caps. & letters from Arthur & Gilbert Scott. Also 2 boxes of socks etc & 1 of bug-powder. I hope I shall never need to use this, but such horrors are common amongst the men tho' Officers, having more shirts etc are able to keep free. Also I received 250 de Reshas from Dad but please ask him to send "Turors" next time & not "American". de Reshe American which arrived are not much good, but anything is a smoke out here, so I didn't mind much. However, please note for

An officer's last letter home before he was to be killed in the August attack at Helles. "I may see you in time to celebrate my 20th birthday at home, tho' as things look at present, there's not much chance of that."

2ND LT. E. DUCKWORTH
(6th Bn. Lancashire Fusiliers)

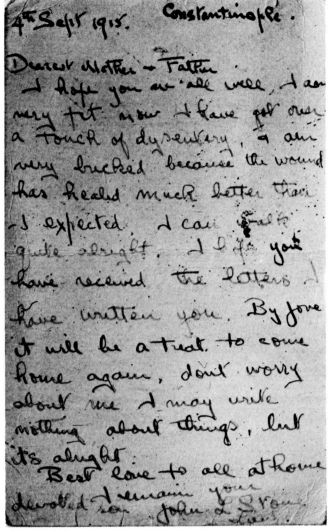

4th Sept 1915.   Constantinople.

Dearest Mother & Father
I hope you are all well, I am
very fit now. I have got over
a touch of dysentery, & am
very bucked because the wound
has healed much better than
I expected. I can walk
quite alright. I do hope you
have received the letters I
have written you. By jove
it will be a treat to come
home again, don't worry
about me. I may write
nothing about things, but
its alright.
     Best love to all at home
devoted I remain your
son   John L Stone.

Constantinople reached in 1915 but not as had been intended! An officer wounded and captured in August writes to his parents in London.

SIR LEONARD STONE
(Lt. 4th Bn. Worcester Regiment)

Captured British "Dardanelles and Gallipoli" officers photographed in Turkey. Seated L to R: Lt. Cdr. A. D. Cochrane, Captain Cedric Coxon, Lt. J. L. Stone, Capt. R. D. Ellcot and 2nd Lt. W. G. S. Fawkes. In the row to the rear: Lt. Stephen White is 2nd on the left, Lt. John Still is next to the right, then Lt. J. M. Entwistle and next but one is Captain H. P. Dyson.

SIR LEONARD STONE

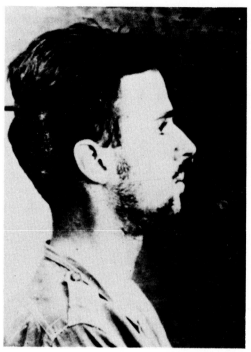

A September 1918 Turkish police H.Q. photograph of Lt. Leonard Stone
on his recapture after an attempted escape.

After his unsuccessful escape attempt Lieutenant Stone and a fellow
escapee wrote notes to assist in the corroboration of each other's
statement. The notes were exchanged in the prison toilet.

"I can't understand any men striking at a time like this." A Gallipoli view of the Home Front, but the writer notes too that war profits are being made.

A. E. Bumpuss (*Lt. R.E.*)

Egyptian Labour Corps at work, X beach.

B. H. PAIN
Surgeon R.N.D.

Copied from a propaganda message to the Turks. Note the Asquithian exhortation!

MAJOR W. G. HOLE

TO THE TURKS.

OSMANLI — E.

BUYURUN. KORKU. YOK.

BIZ INGLISI TE' ESSUF OSMANLI-E IJERIM

BIZ INGLISI DAIMA OSMANLIE DOSTANE, LAKIN

ONLAR ALEMANE OSMANLIYE DOGRU DUSHMANE

DOGRHU DIR!

BEKLE VE GYUR

Come inside — you will be safe.
We English are sorry for the Turks,
We English always friendly to the Turks, but these
Germans are enemies to the Turks.
It is true
Wait and See —

En route for the new offensive and a landing at Suvla Bay

Sir Ian Hamilton did receive reinforcements, but only in July and August were they to be in numbers offering the Commander in Chief the opportunity to make a new plan to break the deadlock. German U boats in the Mediterranean presented a considerable threat to these men on their way out to the Dardanelles. In this photo, body and soul seem to be under care (the former with life jackets) as Yeomanry troops attend a troopship service.

LORD NATHAN

An upturned lifeboat and survivors of the troopship *Royal Edward* torpedoed in the Aegean on 13 August with the loss of over 850 lives. *Royal Edward* was bringing reinforcements to the Peninsula. The hospital ship *Soudan* is taking these men aboard.

J. G. T. TAYLOR
(Surgeon R.N.V.R.)

The August offensive at Anzac

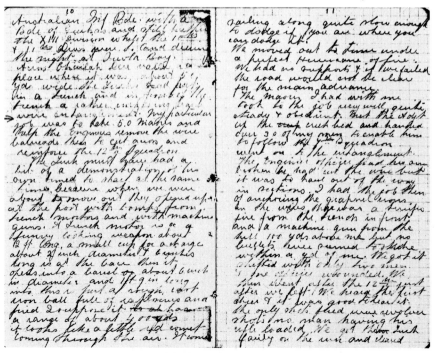

Sir Ian Hamilton's August plan was for diversionary assaults at Helles and on the right and centre of the line at Anzac. This was to assist in a move north along the beach at Anzac, then to file up three unreconnoitred gullies in an attempt to outflank the Turkish positions on the heights above. To be coordinated with this was a new landing on the open beaches still further north at Suvla Bay. A trooper in the Otago Mounted Rifles N.Z.E.F. describes the night advance on the Turkish outposts defending the approach to the Chailak Dere, one of the gullies selected for the allied outflanking attack at Anzac.

M. A. RICHARDS

A New Zealand officer of the Otago Mounted Rifles has had responsibility for assisting in the clearing away of some of the wire obstructions blocking the way up one of the gullies for the night attack. This officer criticises the tactics being employed and later in his diary he makes scornful comments on the performance of non regular British units. Such comments find an echo quite frequently in the papers of Australians. The failure at Suvla was usually at the root of such criticism, but the failure here was really one for which the senior commanders were mainly responsible, not the regimental officers, N.C.O.s and men.

MAJOR F. M. TWISLETON

It was a magnificent achievement to reach Chunuk Bair, the summit of the most vital ridge at Anzac, but the Turks brought up reinforcements in time to prevent success being won by the attackers. It had proved impossible to dig effective cover in the hard stony ground, field telephone wires had been repeatedly destroyed by shelling and to add to these problems misdirected allied artillery shelled the New Zealanders in this precarious position. Together with Gurkhas and U.K. troops, the New Zealanders fought desperately to hold Chunuk Bair. "Our casualties are enormous and we are holding on desperately . . . we have neither food nor water."

A. Bayne
(Bugler. 1st Bn. Wellington Regiment, N.Z.E.F.)

Wounded after the opening day of the August offensive from Anzac.

A. E. Robinson
(Pte. 1st Bn. Auckland Regiment, N.Z.E.F.)

at 4.30 pm the mighty bombardment by heavy Naval guns Howitzers field & Mountain guns began, & for an hour they hammered away to some purpose & meanwhile every possible enemy gun was replying the noise was terrific the danger considerable & the damage to trenches was rather heavy some casualties also [Enemy this of course was inevitable] Our Artillery ceased suddenly at 5-30 & then at the given sound of three whistles the brave irresistible conquering heroes of the 2nd 3rd & 4th Battln's sprung out like bloodhounds released from their leash, over the parapets & straight for the Turks trenches (each man only carried his rifle & bayonet 200 rounds of ammunition his waterbottle & two hand biscuits) they rushed over the open ground in the face of a hellish fire from shrapnel, machine & rifle fire & alas many a brave man bit the dust but over they went the first lot into the 3rd trench the 2nd lot into the 2nd trench & the last lot (that had the most deadly time of all in crossing) into the 1st trench where a desperate hand to hand struggle ensued in each line of trenches. The Austns did deadly work with the bayonet till the sight of that charge is one it can never fade from a man's memory who witnessed it.

The battle for Lone Pine, which opened in the evening of 6 August, was launched as a major diversion from the planned operations on the left of the Anzac positions. Attacking across open ground, in some places emerging from tunnels dug beneath no-man's land, the Australians found themselves confronted with heavy pine-log roofed trenches. These were exceptionally difficult to enter from above, though some success was achieved by over-running the trench and bombing a way in through the communication trenches. Salvation Army Padre McKenzie writes to Commissioner James Hay at Melbourne, Victoria, and goes on to describe the aftermath of the battle. In the trenches "Hundreds upon hundreds of dead Turks lay and many Australians. In some cases the dead lay on top of the wounded. They were three layers deep in places. They couldn't be removed just then and we had to carry the wounded over the dead. . . ." On the following day diversionary attacks at the NEK led to what may sadly be considered the most tragically fruitless losses of all, when Australians of the 8th and the 10th Light Horse were simply mown down as each wave went into its ordained attack.

CAPT. W. McKENZIE

Turkish prisoners captured in the August offensive being escorted by
Indian troops along the beach to Anzac Gully.

A. W. Ross
(Australian Postal Corps.)

Newly landed mail at Anzac after the August offensive. It is stored in a gully and awaits mule delivery to separated Australian, New Zealand, British and Indian units.

A. W. Ross
(*Australian Postal Corps.*)

6/7 August: the landing at Suvla Bay

5th   All barrows, down, unwr[?] packed. Felt very sick. Went to Doctor & had to tie up all day. Medicine worked wonders. Kits etc packed

6th   Ready to move off at 8 am Went to [?] head. with spare underclothing. Moved off at 5pm. Embarked at 7pm. Voyage uneventful until we arrived at Suvla Bay

7th   4.30 am Heard heavy cannonade, and found our ship under shell fire. Neighbouring vessel hit. Turkish Artillery very heavy and our infantry advance magnificently in the face of it. Our cruisers shell enemy batteries eventually silencing them. We landed on northern spur of the bay having to wade to shore. Whaled barrow towards HQ. Had to act as Signal clerk all night very cold. Infantry made splendid advance No 4 Wagon under fire. Terrific rain. General Mahon challenged

Into battle with a barrow and spare underclothing: a signaller at the Suvla landings. The senior command of the United Kingdom New Army troops, and then the Territorials who followed them, seems not fully to have appreciated that speed of movement inland was vital to the success of the whole plan of operations, though Sir Ian Hamilton had given explicit orders to this effect. The line of hills which rimmed the flatness of the plain inland of the beaches was not swiftly stormed, even the slight isolated elevations in the plain were not taken quickly, and all that the great scheme produced was a new stalemate with an added geographical location.

J. C. DART

Troops embarking aboard H.M.S. *Theseus* for the Suvla landing. The men are probably from the 6th Battalion East Yorks (Pioneers).

LT. F. JAQUES
(Engineer Lieutenant. R.N.)

August: the monitor H.M.S. *Roberts* supports the Suvla operations.

CDR. C. H. LONGDEN GRIFFITHS

A naval padre's first experience of action as the monitor H.M.S. *Raglan* supports with shellfire the operations at Suvla and Anzac.

THE REV. A. C. WHITE

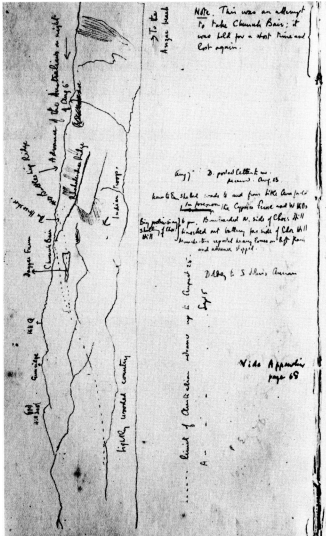

Queuing for water: Suvla. The lack of adequate provision for water supply to troops in the intense heat of summer caused great hardship and some indiscipline.

E. H. DIXON
(Squadron Sergeant Major. Middlesex Yeomanry)

Plenty of horses and plenty of ships but not plenty of time. Suvla in August.

W. A. YOUNG
(87th Bde. Field Ambulance)

orders to stand to arms at 4. a. m.   Had some water
& biscuits — no fires allowed.

Tuesday, 10th August
Stood to arms at 4. a. m.   The 53rd Division are to
attack hills round Anna farta & we are to support the
attack.   Shrapnel again this morning.   Got some
straw to lie on last night, so did not feel so cold.   We
have not even burberrys with us.   Snipers in trees
hard at work again — one Turk was painted to represent
a pig.   We brought down 3 snipers out of trees.
Moved off at 10.30. a. m. to do a general attack.   We
soon came under a heavy fire, but we went on & on.
We had an awful time & lost heavily.   Capt. Patou &
2nd Lt. Oliver were killed, & Major Karsey was badly
wounded, also our Company Commander was wounded
(compound fracture of leg)   We finally got to a line &
dug ourselves in for the night, but were hotly
attacked on 2 sides, the Turks on one side shouting
"Cease fire, we are Gurkhas".   We re opened & they
retired.   I saw Sgt. Lyno of Accomb who is in the
Y. & L. regt. he was most brave, & I saw him
shot through the stomach.   He would not get
into the trench.   I was in, but he sat outside &
brought down many Turks.   I hope he recovers,
his last words to me were "Do you know Old Richardson
of Accomb is dead"?   We were ordered to

Snipers at Suvla. "One Turk was painted to represent a pig." A
contemporary account from an officer in the 8th Battalion Northumber-
land Fusiliers draws attention to the threat posed by snipers in front of
the positions reached by the British troops.

Lt. Col. C. H. Lindberg

The trees from which camouflaged sniper observers had to be shot. Hill
971 in the distance. Photograph taken from 3rd County of London
Yeomanry trenches.

Capt. J. N. Mankin
(Tpr. 3rd County of London Yeomanry)

18 August: Middlesex Yeomanry aboard a "Beetle" bound for Suvla Bay.

E. H. Dixon

21 August, Suvla: crossing the Salt Lake towards Chocolate Hill

A major advance at Suvla was planned for 21 August. The Regular Army 29th Division, which had distinguished itself at Cape Helles, was now in the line at Suvla to play a part in the attack. In the large-scale costly and unsuccessful advance which was attempted, one element was the crossing of the openly exposed dry Salt Lake towards the allied positions near where the main advance was to be launched. This was necessary to reinforce Chocolate Hill, a small rise on the approach to the hills which dominated the central stage of this battle, taking place in an amphitheatre where the vital seats were occupied by the Turks. In this photograph soldiers fill their water-bottles before setting off on what would be, in every sense, a hot day's work.

E. H. DIXON

The 2nd County of London Yeomanry falling in for the advance across the Salt Lake: 2 p.m. 21 August, Lala Baba, Suvla Bay.

MAJOR H. FELLOWES PRYNNE
(2nd County of London Yeomanry)

21 August: Lieutenants Crocker and Marsden of the 3rd County of London
Yeomanry under shell fire crossing the Salt Lake.

Capt. J. N. Mankin

21 August: the Yeomanry cross the Salt Lake at Suvla.

C. H. Jenkinson

21 August: Suvla Bay after the advance. Discarded equipment in the foreground, Salt Lake to left, Chocolate Hill in centre.

MAJOR H. FELLOWES PRYNNE
(Cpl. 2nd County of London Yeomanry)

from a beach of multi-coloured shingle into a sky-blue sea and on the afternoon of Aug. 21st advanced, acting in reserve to troops which were assaulting the Turkish trenches but, being of course daylight, exposed to the enemy's guns.

We trudged forward ~~under~~ for over 2½ miles, over a mile of which was swept by shrapnel fire, the shells falling all round us & men ~~falling in every direction~~; while over our heads the good old ironclads pumped shell after shell ~~back~~ in answer. The hills in the distance were just huge crackling mounds of rifle fire ~~with~~ while here & there the sharp, insistent rapping of the machine guns ~~were~~ was heard. The ground was covered in places with dry gorse & stunted trees which caught fire & ~~burned~~ crackled fiercely. Many of the wounded had crawled under these bushes thinking in a frenzy of pain that they would afford protection ~~instead~~ instead of which the fires spread & they were ~~found~~ burnt to death, sometimes past all

The daylight crossing of the Salt Lake at Suvla under enemy fire on 21 August. A trooper writes of his experience. The final sentence continues on the following sheet to read: "Burnt to death sometimes past all recognition."

C. W. BRAND
(London Yeomanry)

21 August: Chocolate Hill reached.

E. H. DIXON

Major Llewellyn of the 3rd County of London Yeomanry surveys the Suvla scene from Chocolate Hill.

CAPT. J. N. MANKIN

3rd County of London Yeomanry dug in on Chocolate Hill.

Capt. J. N. Mankin

Middlesex Yeomanry in Suvla trenches.

E. H. Dixon

Middlesex Yeomanry enjoy a tobacco issue.

E. H. Dixon

Some formalities preserved. Yeomanry officers take a meal in Suvla.

Lord Nathan

Turkey trot: the curse of dysentery

143

Casualty clearing station: approaches to Suvla.

Dr. W. E. Chadwick
(2nd Lt. 1/7 Essex)

Sergeant Kersnell and Squadron Sergeant
Major Dixon of the Middlesex Yeomanry in
trenches at Suvla.

E. H. Dixon

Middlesex Yeomanry ration dump: Green Hill, Suvla.

E. H. Dixon

Heat, flies, open latrines, unburied men and mules, impure water and unsuitable food all played their part in bringing disease, which was a drain on physical capacity and the resilience of morale. Dysentery in some measure affected virtually all troops. "Passing blood and slime" was one diarist's graphic description, but perhaps even this does not convey the dispiriting hopelessness which afflicted the sufferers. In this letter the writer only refers to the necessary use of his notepaper for the urgent latrine visit, but in a letter written a week later, Frank Waring complains of worsening diarrhoea and noted that lice of "all colours and pedigree have evacuated". His reference seems to imply that rats were leaving a sinking ship.

FRANK E. WARING
(6th Manchesters)

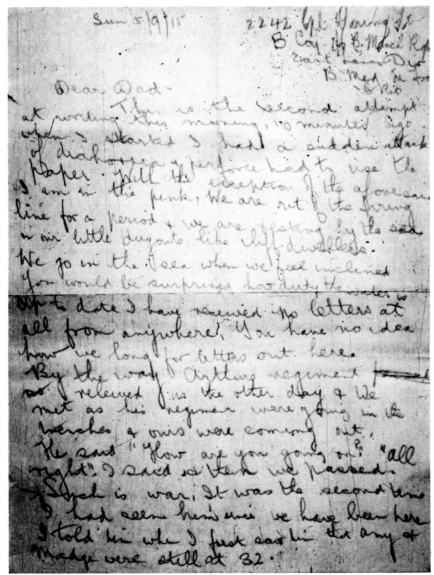

17. Oct "The outlook here now, does not appear to be particularly rosy. With the prospect of winter coming on. Very little progress has been made for a long time despite the optimistic outlook of the press.
The political situation in the Balkans has reached a crisis & much depends on what attitude Rumania takes. If she decides or gets bribed in throwing her lot in with Germany. the Galipoli expedition must fail. Our forces would have to keep a look out for Egypt & India. It will certainly be a loss of prestige, if nothing worse

28 Oct We arrived off Cape Helles this morning having come direct from Malta. After conveying a over 800 invalids from Anzac & Suvla. The place has considerably altered in aspect since last here. Where once was scrub & grass is now absolutely bare. It is honeycombed "dug outs" are everywhere, roads are cut leading to all important points. Telegraph wires are rigged up everywhere just like one sees in the country at home. Shells are continually coming across from the Asiatic side & from the opposite direction. A railway Tender. "Fama" this evening had to shove off from the

A sick berth steward of the hospital ship *Soudan* records the toll of sickness on the Peninsula at the same time as a new campaign in the Eastern Mediterranean is being mounted at Salonika. The steward is not to know that the Kitchener visit he notes will lead to top level approval of the new Commander in Chief's decision to evacuate the Gallipoli Peninsula.

W. G. OLVER

not so perhaps the efforts of the destroyer were simply due to elation of spirit.

This afternoon visited the Diarrhoea Rest Camp & took my confirmation candidates for the last class in preparation for the Communion. On the former place some quite young lads who no doubt their campaign has altered their for life. One only hopes it is really so, & that a fresh start made out here will be maintained afterwards at home.

No attempt whatever was made to celebrate the day. Threatened to have Canada's day, it but it is, let it die out and come off.

Inspiration for those in desperation. A padre visits his confirmation candidates in the "Diarrhoea Rest Camp".

RT. REV. J. C. WAND

The November storm

WAR DIARY
or
INTELLIGENCE SUMMARY
(Erase heading not required.)

Army Form C. 2118

Instructions regarding War Diaries and Intelligence
Summaries are contained in F. S. Regs., Part II.
and the Staff Manual respectively. Title Pages
will be prepared in manuscript.

Place	Date	Hour	Summary of Events and Information	Remarks and references to Appendices
Gallipoli Peninsula	Nov 26		Quiet night.	
		1400	COs conference at Bde. Hdqrs after which the Brigadier took the COs round the second line, and also gave orders that by Sunday all officers should have visited second line.	
		1700	Very severe thunderstorm, with very strong gale, and torrents of rain.	
		2000	All Telephone communication was cut off, and all dug-outs flooded out.	
		2100	Reported to Bde Hqr. that all trenches were flooded, water had come in as though it had been a tidal wave. That many men must have been drowned, and few had been able to save their rifles and equipment. The men were standing up to their knees in water, behind the parados of the trenches. Orders were received for to dig in behind the parados, and that the line had to be held at all costs	W.

1875. Wt. W593/426 1,000,000 4/15 J.B.C. & A. A.D.S.S./Forms/C. 2118.

Place	Date	Hour	Summary of Events and Information	Remarks and references to Appendices
Gallipoli Peninsula	Nov 27th	2100 (cont)	Soon after midnight telephone communication was established between Bn and Bde. Reports sent to Bde informing that the trenches were in bad condition, the cold being intense, and the heavy rain and cold wind continuing. By daylight the men who were capable of work had thrown up for themselves in most cases sufficient cover to protect them from shrapnel fire. The water had subsided in the trenches to an average of 4 feet. A few overcoats, rifles and a certain amount of ammunition were recovered. Great difficulty was experienced in bringing up rations for the men, but eventually Bully Beef, a few biscuits and a little rum, issued. The conditions during the day were trying, men were huddled together in shallow trench, dug behind the parados during the night with any implements they could lay their hands on. Any who walked about stood a great risk of being shot, in fact during the day casualties were fairly heavy, from the snipers. A great deal of shrapnel was fired during the day, chiefly at parties of men who were given permission to leave the trenches, all in various states of exhaustion, to go to the ambulance. Of these there is	

1875. Wt. W593/426 1,000,000 4/15 J.B.C. & A. A.D.S.S./Forms/C. 2118.

Place	Date	Hour	Summary of Events and Information	Remarks and references to Appendices
Gallipoli Peninsula	Nov 27th (cont)		no doubt a great number who failed to reach the ambulances, and died from exhaustion on the way. A cold N.E wind blew all day, with a little rain and sleet at intervals, and it is feared that a great number of men died from exposure. Towards evening the weather got worse, developing into a snow blizzard, with intense cold, and men were still struggling down to the ambulances in large quantities.	

November: icy rain and biting winds, flooded trenches, intense cold and then a blizzard wrought havoc among men already weakened by dysentery. Some measure of the misery caused may be gauged by the total of 280 deaths and 16,000 cases of frostbite resulting from a "natural" rather than a manmade calamity. The war diary of the 86th Brigade, 29th Division.

28 November: Anzac.

Dr. W. E. Chadwick
(2nd Lt. 1/7 Essex)

A transformed landscape: Anzac under snow.

Brig. J. G. McNeill

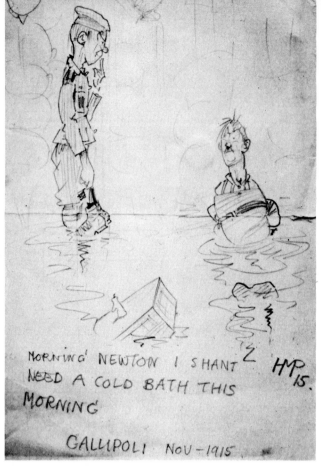

Humour even in the middle of the November floods.

Rt. Rev. J. C. W. Wand

In the storm an officer of the 14th Sikhs writes of the privations suffered by Sikhs, Gurkhas and the Turks of whom: "we shot as many as possible, poor devils".

Lt. Gen. Sir Reginald Savory

The evacuation of Anzac and Suvla: completed 20 December

Salvaging on the shore after storms in October have wrecked Watson's Pier at Anzac. This photograph taken before the more severe storm still in November provides an illustration of one problem to be considered in any seaborn evacuation. Evacuation of Anzac and Suvla was authorised on 7 December, but on-the-spot planning had begun a fortnight earlier. The danger of the Turks advancing on a reduced, overcrowded beachhead while it was actually being evacuated, had to be avoided, and this was achieved by plans which quite brilliantly deceived the Turks so that they did not realise that evacuation was taking place.

A. W. Ross
(*Australian Postal Corps.*)

Dummy guns constructed by the Navy being taken to Suvla to assist in the deception plans concealing the intention of evacuation.

Capt. H. M. Denham *R.N.*

Orders for the evacuation of Suvla. "Even adhere to some extent to the favourite custom of appearing on the skyline."

Lt. Col. A. L. Cameron
(*2nd Lt. R.F.A.*)

personnel left over from the Intermediate Stage, but the embarkation of further guns, animals, matériel and stores, will cease, except as regards guns which it is found possible to remove.

(4) The possibility of the Turk commencing an attack during any period of the evacuation must be kept constantly in mind. Such attacks will become more likely as the evacuation proceeds, but much depends on our succeeding in preventing the enemy discovering that such an operation is in progress.

(5) During the Intermediate and Final Stages every possible means to deceive the enemy must be utilized. The gun and S.A. ammunition expended must be normal. The usual fires will be lit by day and by night, especially in areas evacuated by batteries or battalions, and all will be ordered to show themselves in the vicinity of old camps and bivouacs, and even adhere to some extent to the favourite

custom of appearing on the sky line. All officers concerned are to be warned as to the necessity for the early evacuation of documents and records, and for the destruction of all papers not so removed.

(6) Throughout the course of the final stage boats will be lying off the shore at points where stragglers or wounded men may come down to the beach.

(7) MEDICAL During the final stage lightly wounded cases must embark with the fighting troops.
Two hospital lighters will be provided at SUVLA for the conveyance of badly wounded cases to hospital ships.

Cf Fuller

Lieut. Colonel. G.S.
29th Division

Issued at 0900. 13/1/15!
Copy No 1 G.S. 29th Div
2 A.A. & Q.M.G.
3 58th F.A. Bde.
4 R.E.
5 86th Inf Bde

guard, which judging by the firing were discovered before they embarked. Considering that at the Rhododendron Ridge our trenches were only 35 yards away from the Turks it is very wonderful they were not discovered before. By 5.0 everybody was off & at daylight we opened fire on the advance parties of the Enemy who had discovered the absence of everybody & had started an enormous shrapnel display all along the beach (which they have a very accurate range of), I suppose this was to show us what they could have done if they had discovered earlier, it was certainly no good for anything else as everybody was well away from the beach & out of range. The success of the show rather takes away the bitter taste, the abandonment of the place, gives one —

I hear all our mails are to be delayed 8 days in order we shall not let people at home know so that by the time you get this you will know all the details & most probably find a lot of my statements wrong.

Most of the other ships have returned to harbour & left two of us "blister" & one or two monitors out to worry the Turks as they start taking over what was for 4 months been part of the British Empire.

I don't think there is anything in above likely to be of use to the Enemy, so suppose I can pass the censor.

Have been up all night but so am not feeling very bright.

Very best love to you all

Fro

Frank.

10.0 p.m.
Have just arrived. We are very
in harbour.
The first ship to leave to
arrive of the convoy
+ to land its embarkation. the
they have hoisted over
everyone flag over
hole today.

19, 20 December: this letter was written in two stages while the Anzac Suvla evacuation was being conducted. The earlier part of the letter is full of foreboding for the morrow despite the work accomplished on the 18th, but this engineer officer was able to conclude the letter with an account of the astonishing degree of success achieved.

F. JAQUES
(Engineer Lieutenant R.N.)

started bombarding our trenches not very long though. Just before daylight we manned the stations, ready to fire on the Turks if they came down, but they hadn't woken up to the fact yet so we fired one or two shells among the tents we had left to burn them and then we went back to Imbros.

21st

The soldiers had a lot of different dodges for making the Turks think they were still in the trenches after they had left, rifles fired by candles burning or drops of water filling a bucket and a gramaphone that was started by a candle burning away. The captains Generals and admirals, thanked each other all round and generally patted each other on the back, Two captains R.N. were particularly thanked. I suppose it is about the most successful or only successful bit of staff work during the war. They Telegraphed at once to let the papers know before the

20 December: "They telegraphed at once to let the papers know before the Germans publish it as a defeat." A midshipman of H.M.S. *Chatham* writes of the successful evacuation of the troops from Suvla Bay.

CDR. T. S. FOX PITT

PENINSULA PRESS.

No. 95.   MONDAY, JANUARY 3rd, 1916.   Official News.

The Evacuation of Suvla—Anzac.

Seen through German glasses.

We are indebted to the German wireless telegrams for a most interesting, and quite new account of our last days in the Suvla—Anzac area. Comment is unnecessary, as the details speak for themselves. According to this account, which purports to be that of eye-witnesses who have arrived at Salonika, "the English ... during and Anafarta to break through the Turkish lines, aided throughout the day by the continuous fire of their guns on land and on shipboard: this attack was repulsed by the brave and heroic Turkish troops, and therefore on the night of the 19th—20th Dec. the flight of the English commenced—a flight which was observed by the Turks at 3 a.m. The Turks inflicted gigantic losses on the English and took spoils that extended for kilometres, including poker cards, whisky flasks, enormous quantities of corned beef, jam, cocoa, soda water, lemon juice—these from the officers quarters—not to mention such things as electrical installations, ambulance wagons, spare wheels, complete wireless apparatus, etc." A recently captured Turkish prisoner has just informed us that the Turkish Commander has been decorated as a reward for this victory.

Local News.

HELLES.—The chief item of news in the Helles area is the successful operation carried out on the 29th December by the 52nd Division, which resulted in the gain of Turkish trenches and the capture of 26 prisoners, apart from a considerable number of the enemy overwhelmed by the explosion of two of our mines. We have consolidated our gains and apparently instilled such a wholesome respect for us among the enemy in that section, that, though they were seen to fix bayonets they would not leave their trenches.

SALONIKA.—During the last week we have extended our lines so that they now run from the river Vardar on the West, with our left flank resting on the marshes that extend as far as the sea along both banks of the river. The extreme East of our line is on the Gulf of Orfano where the stream that takes off the waters of Lake Beshik enters the sea; and the distance from the Gulf of Orfano to a point some 7 or 8 miles due North of the town of Salonika gives a line of approximately 40 miles, running almost due East and West, to be held by the Allied troops. More than half of this front of 40 miles lies along the Southern shores of the two lakes of Beshik and Aivisal. Outer lines of defence have been prepared further to the North of Salonika, and the whole forms a very strong fortress. Indeed, in the opinion of the French General Castelnau, who has just paid a visit of inspection, it is an impregnable fortress. The Peninsula of Chalcidice with its three promontories jutting out like fingers is varied in character and affords complete room and excellent manoeuvre ground for a large army.

At present all the high mountains to the North of Salonika and the Peninsula of Chalcidia are snow covered, rendering military operations difficult. The Easternmost finger of the Peninsula has a double interest from its past and present associations. Xerxes, King of Persia, having under his command no mean army, even reckoned by modern standards (Herodotus gives it as 2,600,000 soldiers, and as many non-combatants or Camp followers, and Greek and Egyptian "Labor Corps") caused a canal to be dug across the narrow neck of the isthmus to spare his fleet the dangerous passage round the promontory of Mt. Athos. In Medieval and Modern times the promontory of Mt. Athos has constituted a semi-independent religious enclave peopled with the inmates of numerous monasteries of the Eastern Church, with a subsidiary population of Greek and Bulgarian cut throats who have sought its sanctuary. No female, of the human or brute kind, may live within the enclave; and so strict is the rule that the monks have to import even the eggs necessary for their ascetic mode of life.

GALICIA.—A great battle is now proceeding in Eastern Galicia on the Middle Strypa between the Russians and Austrians; nothing is known of the result as yet. Also in the Adriatic, off Cattaro, the Allied Fleet (possibly including British cruisers) encountered an Austrian Naval Division and put it to flight; the Austrians lost two ships.

MESOPOTAMIA—Troops are being steadily pushed up to reinforce General Townshend.

The Turkish Government has become seriously anxious about their position at Baghdad and has hurried troops over to that front. Distances are great in Mesopotamia and the rate of travelling necessarily slow. It takes, under ordinary conditions, about three weeks to move a Division to Baghdad from Mossul, the next important military centre upriver. The Turks, if they use river transport, have the advantage of the current which is swift, but above Baghdad the Tigris is only navigable for light craft, rafts of inflated skins being the usual method of transport.

It must always be remembered that the possession of Baghdad (with Kerbela) as the ancient capital of the Caliphs is of more importance to the prestige of the Turks than any other Moslem city, with the possible exception of Mecca and Constantinople.

CHINA.—Apparently, from reports received from the Far East, the Republican party is not going to watch the passing of the Republic, from which they had hoped so much, without raising a forcible protest against the establishment of a new Monarchy. The Province of Yunnan has already declared its independence, and other provincial Governments may follow suit. The Central Government is satisfied as to the loyalty of the other provinces and will send troops against the revolutionaries. When the Mahomedans of Yunnan rebelled some years ago the province was "pacified" by the extermination of nine tenths of the whole Moslem population.

The troops at Cape Helles would get this Mediterranean Expeditionary Force news-sheet in which G.H.Q. report (or invent) a German-Turkish account of the Anzac Suvla evacuation, an account which was of course strikingly different from the remarkably successful operation which had in fact taken place. No losses had been incurred except of face and of stores.

A. GILLOTT
(R.N.D.)

Anzac resting place for those who would be left behind.

DR. W. E. CHADWICK
(2nd Lt. 1/7 Essex)

The evacuation of Cape Helles: completed 8/9 January 1916

It seemed much less likely that similar success could be achieved at Cape Helles after the decision was taken that complete evacuation of the Peninsula was a necessity. Apart from troop reinforcements, the Turks were now calling upon heavier artillery and more ammunition reaching them from Germany via the new German-Turkish ally Bulgaria. Deception again had to be planned, increasing Turkish military activity had to be countered at the very time the beach-head was being thinned out for final evacuation. Here, late in the campaign, *River Clyde* is attracting shellfire as she did from first to last.

A. M. PATERSON
R. E. attached to R.N.D.

Unhappy landings. Christmas Day at Cape Helles, Hunter Weston Hill.

SURGEON LT. B. H. PAIN

A Nieuport 10 in a dispersal pen: Helles, January 1916.

G. S. LESLIE

O.C. London
¼ Co RE   S=CRET.

Orders as to Evacuation.

1. It is essential that Officers and NCOs who will form part of the garrison on the last night should be thoroughly acquainted both by day & night with the particular route which they will have to follow.
The above orders concern — as far as I know at present — only the London & Lowland Field Coys, & perhaps in their case only such Detcht as they leave behind to lay trip bombs.

2. Watches must be most carefully synchronised, & the time will be circulated from Corps H.Q. at least twice during daylight on the last day.

3. All troops will proceed to MUDROS except Corps H.Q.

4. During the 1st period — which is now actually in progress — all sick and weakly men, and all superfluous materials, stores, supplies, and ammn. will be removed

5. The final period will last 48 hours, during the 1st night of which all personnel & material will be removed except the absolutely last party to go (trip bomb party)

6. It is extremely important that bivouacs etc must be left so as to give the impression that they are occupied; empty boxes should be placed where full ones were. tarpaulins must not be removed

7. In the final march back special precaution must be taken that no sound of our movements is heard by the enemy. No talking near it fine. — no noise of footsteps.

8. All wheels must be removed from [?] left behind, either evacuated, destroyed, or sunk in the sea.

9. Every man embarking will carry one own rations

[signature] Lt Col.
CRE

Evacuation orders. Points are made concerning deception of the Turks, the need for silence during evacuation procedure and then in this document just one detail in what was to be a wholesale destruction of stores and equipment.

REX PALMER
R.E.

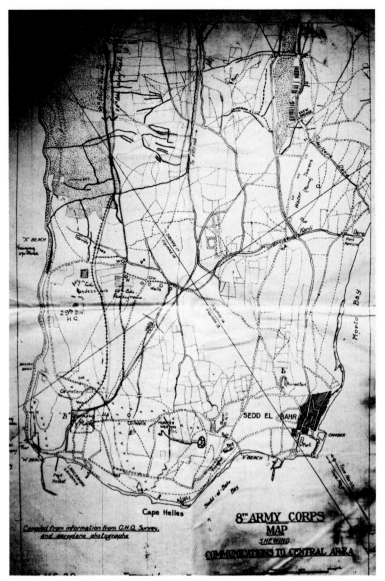

Cape Helles evacuation routes. The map of an engineer officer with responsibility for evacuation procedure.

REX PALMER
R.E.

They also serve who only stand stiff as dummies. R.N.D. Engineer-prepared figures to man the trenches during the last hours of the Cape Helles evacuation.

CAPT. E. F. WETTERN

Breakfast in Sergeants Mess. M. with Stout
Ainsworth & Forbes round latters' Sector.
Down cliff between De Totts & Kereves &
round coast—JANVIER quite exposed in
places but never any firing owing to
weird sort of armistice. French & Turkish
8. SAMEDI! S. Lucien   8-358
Flags on trees in open. Took photos in
front of firing line. Stone parapets—
olives—pictursque firing line. Round
redoubt & back Thompson's route.
Lunch.—Stew a la Hodesdon—barley&
cream. Finishing touches with Stout.
Ev. THE DAY. Up to Post 3 (firing line)
2200 with Stout & Rugg. Quiet. Asquith,
Freiburg, West &c there. Hoods on our
left moved out very quietly 2315—didn't
notice them go. Our men (Howes) closed
& moved into Boyau Central, R men firing
till last minute. Straw down & muffled feet
2345 all moved out. We put down crinolines
in front line. Delay at control—ragtime
signalman. Infantry went , —we put
down 2 Umbrella &c in miles (if do,
at supports, then passed Du ezil &
bomb people & waited for them at
Ligne de Rapii barricade. Further wait
at Post II for Thompson. Then all down to
Post 15—Eski—Longish wait for Blake—
barricaded road & put gear on &
proceeded down. Very quiet. Few French
left round Camp des Oliviers. Via Cypres
to Point at Sedd-el-Bahr—then in fours—
slow progress—over beached French
battleship on to destroyer—squashed
like sardines. On board before
2330. Red and — shells from Asie.

Out to sea. Bonfires started
0400 on all beaches, & Turks
started   JANVIER shelling like
blazes & sending up red flares.
— to catch it from out of range.
9. DIMANCHE! S. Marceli. 9-357
Making for Lemnos, then turned
into Kaphalos Harbour at
da____. Transferred to
____ Mars. Filthy boat, with
terrific crowd on board. Mixed
odds & ends of 29th, 13th, 52nd
& RND. Fight for grub—no
room below. Marine band.
Left Kaphalos at dusk. Slept on
deck—anywhere—cold & blowy.

The vital work of the Royal Naval Division Engineers in leaving barbed
wire obstructions ("umbrellas and crinolines") to hinder the progress of
inquisitive Turks as the Peninsula emptied before them. Note the
curious reference to a sector where there seemed to be a Franco-Turkish
no-fighting agreement.

CAPT. E. F. WETTERN

Cocoa and porridge for those evacuated from Helles.
A seaman's diary of H.M.S. *Lord Nelson* at the final
evacuation of the Gallipoli Peninsula.

G. E. KEELER

Sunday 9th Jan 1916

4. am. The fires which have started:
one after another the flare up & grow.
Huge roaring boiling fires! They
are consuming all that we left as
we withdrew. provisions, ammunition,
mines & gear of all kinds. As
they grow, as sudden glows burst into
flares of dazzling brightness, obliterating
in their light the other enormous fires
paling - the great searchlight of Chanak.
Terrific are these explosions, the
great flare must be hundreds of
feet in diameter tongues of flame
& fragments of burning matter are
hurled far beyond the boiling
centre high into the air.
So great was the smoke after one of
these explosions that it blotted out
from our view all the other fires &

even the whole peninsula itself - one
great, ugly, thick mass of brown
thick smoke.   Any luckless
person within hundreds of yards
must surely have been suffocated
for it moved but slowly, growing
in enormity, hideousness.
Now we have received a signal
that a submarine is lurking
within a mile or half of our
anchorage. Will she deem it worth
while to test our "torpedo proof side"?
It is beginning to grow lighter &
the peninsula can be seen a
smoking mass. And we are
not to close or fire ...
Sedel Bahr; the other ...
are to do the same ...
are to fire too ...

A painting of the post-evacuation bombardment of Cape Helles.

M. J. SMITH
(Royal Marine Light Infantry: H.M.S. Edgar)

A chapter closed: the Turks had not been beaten, but history had been made. From a monitor and from an aeroplane the evacuated Cape Helles battleground is observed.

W. M. GARNER
(Chief Petty Officer R.N.A.S.)

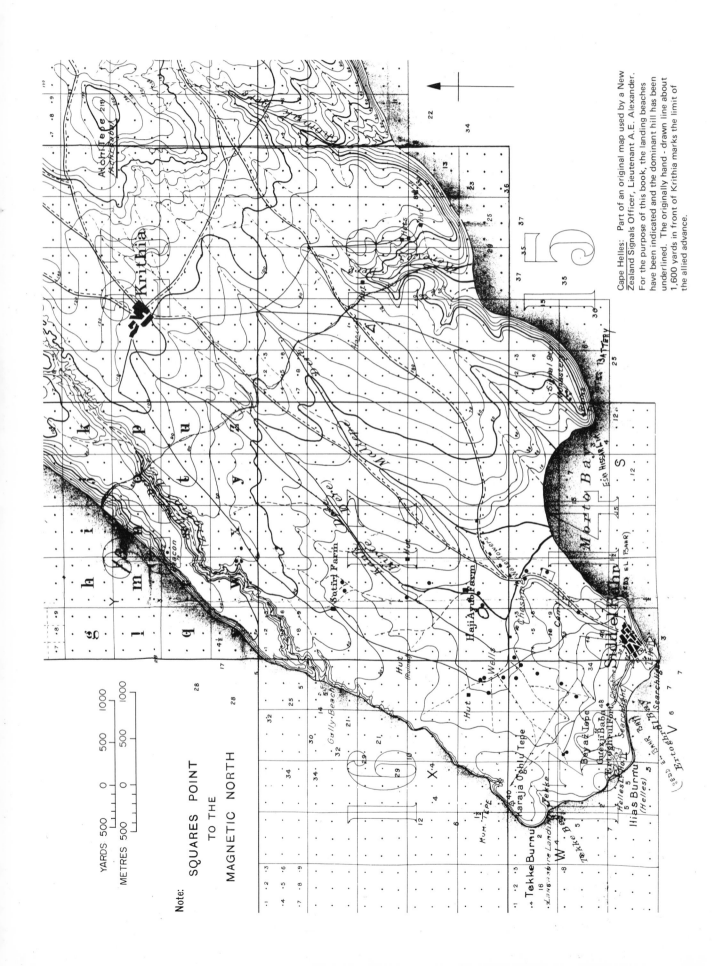

Note:

SQUARES POINT
TO THE
MAGNETIC NORTH

YARDS 500   0   500   1000
METRES 500   0   500   1000

Cape Helles: Part of an original map used by a New
Zealand Signals Officer, Lieutenant A.E. Alexander.
For the purpose of this book, the landing beaches
have been indicated and the dominant hill has been
underlined. The originally hand - drawn line about
1,600 yards in front of Krithia marks the limit of
the allied advance.